DEFYING HITLER

DEFYING HITLER
THE WHITE ROSE PAMPHLETS

Alexandra Lloyd

BODLEIAN
LIBRARY
PUBLISHING

First published in 2022 by the Bodleian Library
Broad Street, Oxford OX1 3BG
www.bodleianshop.co.uk

ISBN 978 1 85124 583 3

Overview, Biographical sketches and Timeline
© Alexandra Lloyd, 2022
Translations © Taylorian Institution, University of Oxford, 2022

The Oxford students' translations of the pamphlets were first
published in *The White Rose: Reading, Writing, Resistance*,
ed. Alexandra Lloyd (Taylor Institution Library, Oxford, 2019)

Every effort has been made to trace copyright holders and to obtain
permission for the use of copyright material (see also p.147); any
errors or omissions will be corrected in future editions of the book.

Publisher: Samuel Fanous
Managing Editor: Deborah Susman
Editor: Janet Phillips
Picture Editor: Leanda Shrimpton
Production Editor: Susie Foster
Cover design by Dot Little at the Bodleian Library
Designed and typeset by Lucy Morton of illuminati
in 9 on 14 Walbaum
Printed and bound by Livonia Print, Latvia,
on 115 gsm vol 1.3 Munken Premium Cream paper

British Library Catalogue in Publishing Data
A CIP record of this publication is available from the British Library

CONTENTS

ACKNOWLEDGEMENTS

This book is the result of collaborative practices of creativity, writing and critical reflection. I wish above all to thank Hildegard Kronawitter and the team at the Weiße Rose Stiftung (White Rose Foundation) in Munich, who have been a tremendous support. I am also grateful to Wolfgang and Emel Huber, Markus Schmorell, Christiane Moll and Jakob Knab for their generous welcome in Munich in November 2019. Many writers and scholars have engaged with the story of the White Rose before me. I wish to acknowledge in particular Christiane Moll's wonderfully detailed work on the lives and writings of Alexander Schmorell and Christoph Probst, and Hinrich Siefken's pioneering work on the resistance pamphlets.

I am indebted to Katherine Hunt and Emily Troscianko for creating regular opportunities to write, and to Tom Herring and Anke Loewensprung for lively and long conversations about the White Rose. Work on the manuscript was made possible by a Knowledge Exchange Fellowship at The Oxford Research Centre in the Humanities (TORCH). The teams at the Bodleian Library and Bodleian Library Publishing have championed and supported the project in many ways and I am especially grateful to Samuel Fanous, Janet Phillips and Leanda Shrimpton.

The translations of texts by the White Rose resistance circle presented here were produced by student members of the White Rose Project, a research and engagement initiative at the University of Oxford: Holly Abrahamson, Zoë Aebischer, Sibylle Bandilla, Sophie Bailey, Lucy Buxton, Ilona Clayton, Luke Cooper, Jonah Cowen, Ro Crawford, James Cutting, Sam Davis, Amelia Farley, Benjy Fortna, Pauline Gümpel, Rachel Herring, Alice Hopkinson-Woolley, Genevieve Jeffcoate, Gerda Krivaite, Lydia Ludlow, Thomas Lyne, Eve Mason, Louise Mayer-Jacquelin, Adam Mazarelo, Beth Molyneux, Timothy Powell, Finn Provan, Amira Ramdani, Poppy Robertson, Emily Rowland, Greta Simpson, Harry Smith, Amy Wilkinson and Madeleine Williamson-Sarll. I am more grateful than I can say to the student translators for their dedication and enthusiasm, and to colleagues for their help and suggestions, especially Jenny Lemke and Jim Reed.

Finally, I wish to thank my family and friends for their love and encouragement, especially Daniel. *Deo gratias!*

A.L., Oxford, May 2021

THE WHITE ROSE: AN OVERVIEW

On Thursday, 18 February 1943, an audience of 14,000 invited guests gathered at the Sports Palace in Berlin. This imposing building, originally an ice rink and later adapted for a variety of large-scale events, had become a popular venue for Nazi rallies, principally thanks to its grand scale. The Reich minister of propaganda, Joseph Goebbels, called it 'Our great political rostrum'.[1] Political spin was certainly needed in February 1943, a disastrous month for the German army, which began with their surrender at Stalingrad on the 2nd. The campaign had cost five months of fighting and 850,000 lives; 91,000 German soldiers had been taken prisoner, of whom over half would be dead by the spring.[2] Meanwhile in North Africa, the Afrika Korps was on the brink of defeat after the Allies had sunk German supply ships on their way to Tripoli in January.

This was the backdrop against which Goebbels addressed the vast crowd in the Sports Palace at around 5 p.m. on 18 February. Above the speakers' podium hung a giant banner emblazoned with the words 'TOTAL WAR — SHORTEST WAR'. In a speech lasting nearly two

Reich minister of propaganda Joseph Goebbels delivers a speech on Thursday 18 February 1943 at the Sports Palace in Berlin. He calls on Germans to support 'total war'.

hours, Goebbels acknowledged the challenges faced on the Eastern Front, stressed the continued threat posed by 'international Jewry' and Bolshevism, and put to his audience the necessity of committing wholeheartedly to 'total war'.[3] This, he argued, would demand all men and women of every class to make even greater sacrifices for the good of the war effort. Reaching the climax of his speech, Goebbels posed a series of ten questions, asking the audience in the Sports Palace to give answer on behalf of their fellow Germans, and so their enemies listening in might hear their responses. 'The English', Goebbels declared, 'maintain that the German people is resisting the government's total war measures. It does not want total war, the English say, but rather capitulation!' Shouts of 'Never!' erupted from the audience. Goebbels continued, 'I ask you: do you want total war? If necessary, do you want a war more total and radical than anything that we can even imagine today?' 'Yes!', the audience enthusiastically responded. Goebbels concluded the speech, his final words drowned out by feverish applause. Afterwards, Goebbels told Albert Speer that this had been politically the best-trained audience in Germany.[4]

This was a carefully orchestrated event, with an audience of fanatically loyal party members, wounded soldiers and prominent figures, including Speer, minister of armaments and munition, who had built a reputation as Hitler's architect. Goebbels claimed in the speech to have been speaking before 'a representative sample of the whole German people, both from the front and the homeland'.[5] The speech had a significant reach: it was broadcast live on national radio, millions of copies were distributed as a pamphlet,[6] and on 24 February excerpts were shown during the *Wochenschau*, the weekly newsreel played in cinemas before every film.

While this spectacle was unfolding in Berlin, some 300 miles away in the southern German city of Munich, a brother and sister in their early twenties sat in cells at the Gestapo prison, awaiting further interrogation. Earlier that day, at around 11 o'clock, Hans Scholl and Sophie Scholl had entered the main building of the Ludwig Maximilian University where they were both students. They had copies of two pamphlets, which they deposited around the atrium at the entrance of the main university building. These pamphlets were part of a series. The sixth, addressed to 'Fellow students!', called for 'freedom and honour', denounced 'Hitler and his cronies' for the devastation at Stalingrad, and urged students to rise up and resist Nazism.

Their clandestine work completed, Hans and Sophie Scholl might have succeeded in their plan to disappear among the many students coming out of lectures, but for a seemingly insignificant act. Sophie, in what she later described in her Gestapo interrogation as the result of either 'high spirits' or 'foolishness',[7] pushed one of the piles of pamphlets over the balustrade and the sheets of paper cascaded down into the empty atrium below. This caught the attention of the university caretaker, Jakob Schmid, who raced up the stairs and apprehended them. The Gestapo were called, the doors to the building locked, and the two students were arrested.[8] Hans and Sophie were taken in handcuffs to the Wittelsbach Palace just under a mile away. Originally a Bavarian royal residence, it had been commandeered and transformed by the Gestapo into the scene of incarceration, interrogation and torture. By the time Goebbels stepped onto the rostrum at the Sports Palace in Berlin, the Scholls were already being interrogated for the second time that day.

Just four days later, on Monday 22 February, Hans and Sophie Scholl were executed by guillotine, alongside another student involved in the group's activities, Christoph Probst, a 23-year-old father of three. Hans was 24 years old; Sophie was 21. A second trial followed on 19 April at which three other core members of the group were sentenced to death and others received prison sentences: 25-year-old student Alexander Schmorell and 49-year-old academic Kurt Huber were executed three months later on 13 July 1943; 25-year-old student Willi Graf was kept in solitary confinement and executed on 12 October. Their crimes were listed as high treason, undermining the troops' morale, and furthering the cause of the enemy through the writing, printing and distribution of pamphlets calling on Germans to mount resistance against Hitler and the National Socialist state.[9]

The White Rose resistance is a household name in Germany, but it is not generally a well-known aspect of the history of the Third Reich elsewhere. The terms 'resistance' and 'World War II' are, in the British imagination, more likely to evoke memories and depictions of French resistance under the Vichy regime and German occupation. When it comes to Germany, we are more familiar with stories of collective guilt and mass collaboration. Yet in the midst of complicity and oppression there *were* attempts at resistance — both violent and non-violent — by those who not only recognized the hatred and corruption inherent in National Socialism but were willing to stand up to it and risk their lives exhorting others to do the same. The individuals involved in the White Rose resistance were familiar with the kind of rhetoric peddled by Goebbels in his 'Total War' speech. Indeed, almost all of them had grown up alongside it, born as they were in the wake of the First World War, educated in National Socialism's systems and required to participate in its youth organizations. As adults, the male students of the White Rose were all conscripted into the army, serving as medical orderlies; Kurt Huber taught at the state-controlled university; and Sophie Scholl participated in compulsory Reich labour service, contributing to the war effort. In this way, they saw at first hand the suffering and persecution of those National Socialism deemed 'unacceptable', how it treated its enemies, and they saw through the propaganda that insisted on viewing fellow human beings as 'subhumans' (*Untermenschen*) or 'life unworthy of life' (*lebensunwertes Leben*).

The story of the White Rose is complex and intricate, with countless twists and turns, and involves a vast network of individuals. Historians have faced significant challenges reconstructing it, due both to the lack of written records and to the need at the time for secrecy, which meant that very little was documented in letters and diary entries, and then mostly through codes or allusions to be deciphered by the recipient. Some of the sources only came to light in the 1990s after the fall of the Berlin Wall, or when family members made private documents accessible to archives or to editors and publishers.[10] The transcripts of the group's interrogation by Gestapo agents are a vital source, but, as 'texts of repression', necessarily need to be treated with care.[11] Under interrogation, stories changed for the protection of others. There are some aspects of the history of which we can never be certain and where we can only imagine thoughts, feelings and deeds. The story of the group's reception has been similarly complex and contested. It is a history that can easily invite partisanship, or appropriation for one cause or another.

My aim here is to provide a short introduction to the individuals at the heart of the White Rose resistance and their writings. Their story is best told when the historical actors speak for themselves, in the resistance pamphlets they wrote, printed and distributed, and in their private correspondence, much of which has never been published in English translation. The reader will, I hope, be inspired to explore their story further, to discover more about these fascinating and remarkable individuals. To this end I have included suggestions for further reading and viewing. The 'Biographical Sketches' chapter offers brief introductions to each of the individuals at the heart of the White Rose circle, though it is important to remember that there were also many others who supported the activities in different ways, many of whom suffered as a result. Even if at times the individuals in the White Rose appear remote, flawed or incomprehensible, they are a timely and hope-filled reminder of the ways in which conscience and moral courage can lead to action that challenges injustice.

FIVE STUDENTS AND AN ACADEMIC

At its broadest, the White Rose resistance incorporated a wide network of individuals who helped to spread the pamphlets and support the core group's endeavours. At its heart were six individuals in Munich: students Hans Scholl, Sophie Scholl, Alexander Schmorell, Christoph Probst and Willi Graf; and Professor Kurt Huber. It is important to understand that their resistance activities were a collective effort, but to call the White Rose a group or movement belies the true nature of their undertakings and the logistics involved. The pamphlet campaign was the result of small friendship groups connecting over time, of individuals reaching out to others, sounding them out with the utmost caution, assessing their safety and reliability. Each individual brought something different to the endeavour, and unlike, for example, Communist resistance groups, they were not bound by a single ideology.[12] The six individuals at the heart of the White Rose did, however, come from similar social backgrounds and had in common upbringings dominated by the pursuit of culture and intellectual exchange. They had all suffered losses of one kind or another: in some cases, the loss of a parent; in others, the loss of security in the family's financial or living situation. These were all individuals who, from childhood onwards, had sought exchange and discourse with others. By the time they took part in the resistance they were united in one thing: that the National Socialist state must be brought down and with it an end to the Second World War. This, they argued, must be done through an appeal to the German people, who in their view had passively permitted Nazism to take root, but who now needed to oppose it from within.

There can be a tendency to think of such people as having been born resistance fighters.[13] That is, of course, not the case. They came to see that the regime was morally bankrupt and became convinced of their own responsibility to act against it, through a combination of their upbringings and encounters with others. Not all of them were even obvious candidates for mounting resistance against National Socialism. Hans Scholl and Sophie Scholl had been relatively enthusiastic members of the Hitler Youth in the 1930s, joining against the wishes of their anti-fascist father.[14] The White Rose members shared a number of common interests, views and values. Among these were a love of culture, of literature, art and music, of nature, and a profound interest in religion and philosophy. In the case of Kurt Huber, these things were also the subject and object of his academic teaching and research.

They read voraciously and widely. Their letters and diaries make frequent mention of the books they were reading, and they sometimes read communally, discussing the ideas they encountered as they went. They read contemporary and ancient literature, banned authors, and texts from across the world. Just as Nazism was attempting to reduce their world-view, they found new worlds through reading and by discussing literature and philosophy with others. The academic Hinrich Siefken has observed that the bulk of their reading 'was imbued

Self-portrait by Sophie Scholl (1921-1943).

with a strong sense of searching for a way out of the chaos'.[15] These were individuals in search of more than the political system in which they lived was willing to give them. Reading their letters and diaries we are confronted with deeply thoughtful and serious individuals, extremely well-read, intelligent and reflective. At the same time, they had a lust for life and for exchange with others. They were joyful, they took pleasure in shared experiences, in the natural world, in evenings with friends at concerts, choir practice, or having drinks in a bar. They were, in essence, quite 'ordinary' people who did extraordinary things.

'MOUNT PASSIVE RESISTANCE!' PAMPHLETS I–IV

By the spring of 1942 the war was going well for Nazi Germany with a string of military successes on both the Western and Eastern fronts. They had conquered France and achieved significant victories in Soviet Russia, launching a summer offensive in May 1942 and capturing the Caucasus. At the same time, Nazi designs for the elimination of enemies it deemed 'subhuman' were also advancing at an accelerated pace. In January the Wannsee Conference was convened to discuss the 'Final Solution' and mass deportations and systematic extermination were being perpetrated across occupied Europe. In March, the concentration camp at Auschwitz, which had been in operation since the outbreak of the war, was expanded.

It was at this moment that all six core members of the White Rose circle found themselves in Munich, the city Adolf Hitler had dubbed the capital of the Nazi movement (*Hauptstadt der Bewegung*). Hans Scholl had begun his studies in medicine at the Ludwig Maximilian University in Munich in the summer semester of 1939 after completing compulsory labour service (*Arbeitsdienst*) and training in the army medical corps. In October 1940 he met Alexander Schmorell, who had transferred from Hamburg to Munich and who was also studying medicine. Christoph Probst was a childhood friend of Alexander Schmorell — they had met at school in 1935 — and had also begun studying medicine in Munich in 1939. He and Hans Scholl met in 1941 through Schmorell. Christoph Probst in turn introduced Willi Graf to the circle in June 1942 after they met at a concert of music by J.S. Bach.[16] Willi Graf had begun studying medicine at the University of Bonn in November 1937. After his preliminary examination the university closed and so he transferred to Munich. In May 1942 he had just returned from ten months' deployment at the front in Russia.[17]

Professor Kurt Huber taught musicology, philosophy and psychology at the university in Munich. His lectures were popular with students, including the members of the White Rose circle. In May 1942 Sophie Scholl was finally able to begin her studies after enduring several months of national labour service. She arrived in Munich in early May in time to celebrate her twenty-first birthday on the 9th with her brother and his friends. There were others in the circle, too, including Traute Lafrenz (b. 1919), who met Hans Scholl through Alexander Schmorell, whom she had come to know when he was at university in Hamburg in the summer of 1939. She was also studying medicine in Munich.

The students spent evenings reading, discussing and exchanging views with each other and with older and more experienced individuals, some of whom became quasi-mentors to the group. They held evening gatherings at the home of Alexander Schmorell's parents in the Harlaching suburb of Munich and in the studio of architect Manfred Eickemeyer (1903–1978), who had been introduced to Hans Scholl by the lawyer Josef Furtmeier (1887–1979).[18] Eickemeyer's work took him to occupied Poland where he witnessed mass shootings of Jews and Poles, information he shared with Hans Scholl and Alexander Schmorell.[19] The students were also invited to attend gatherings organized by the writer-publisher Carl Muth (1867–1944), former editor of the journal *Highland* (*Hochland*), which had been suppressed by the Nazis in 1941. Muth made Hans Scholl's acquaintance through Otl Aicher (1922–1991), a friend of the Scholl family, who would in fact go on to marry his sister, Inge Scholl, in 1952.

At such evenings the students met with dissident and oppositional artists and intellectuals, such as the writer and translator Theodor Haecker (1879–1945), the writer and former actor Sigismund von Radecki (1891–1970) and Professor Kurt Huber. Traute Lafrenz recalled of this time that there seemed to be a 'network of like-minded people, widely cast and finely woven'.[20] On 17 June 1942 the students met at a gathering organized by medical student Otmar Hammerstein (1917–2003) at the home of Viktor Emmanuel Mertens (1895–1974), professor of medicine, and his wife, the pianist and singer Gertrud Mertens (1883–1973). Kurt Huber was also among those who attended. In the course of the evening a discussion sprang up about how, in the current situation, it might be possible to preserve one's inner values. One of the attendees, publisher Heinrich Ellermann (1905–1991), declared that open resistance was pointless, to which Kurt Huber responded: 'Something must be done, and today!'[21] The response of Hans Scholl and Alexander Schmorell to this call to action would become clear in the weeks to come.

The first phase of the White Rose resistance was the writing and dissemination of four pamphlets, in German *Flugblätter*.[22] It is a word that can be traced back to the 1400s and in its etymology suggests speed: these are literally 'flying sheets of paper'.[23] This is apt given the increasing urgency with which the White Rose felt their message needed to reach the German people as the war went on. The first four pamphlets were produced by Hans Scholl and Alexander Schmorell over the course of just sixteen days, between 27 June and 12 July 1942, at the Schmorell family home in Munich.[24] Unpicking and determining the precise authorship from the Gestapo interrogation transcripts, it seems likely that the first and fourth pamphlets were written by Hans Scholl, as well as the first half of the second and third pamphlets. Alexander Schmorell wrote the second half of the second and third pamphlets.[25] Yet this was a collaborative endeavour, as they read and commented on each other's work throughout. Alexander Schmorell later called the pamphlets 'mine and Scholl's intellectual property', reflecting both the fact that they had worked together on the texts and the way in which Schmorell viewed the pamphlets: a result of thought, reflection and creativity.[26] Each text begins with the heading 'Pamphlets of the White Rose' and a corresponding number, suggesting that, from the very beginning, the authors intended to produce a series. Each pamphlet concludes with a variation on the same message, namely instructions to the reader to make and distribute further copies of it. The highly risky and logistically complex process of printing and disseminating the pamphlets was also the result of cooperation.

The origins of the name 'The White Rose' have been much debated over the years. During his interrogation by Gestapo agent Anton Mahler on 20 February 1943, Hans Scholl said that it had been chosen 'at random'; however, he knew that for the pamphlets to be effective propaganda the name would need to sound good and suggest that there was something of a manifesto behind it.[27] It might also be, he added, the result of his having read a book by Clemens Brentano entitled *The White Rose*.[28] Hans Scholl added that the name had no links to the white rose in English history. It has also been suggested that the name had religious connotations, evoking innocence and purity, or as a symbol of the Mother of Christ.[29] When Sophie Scholl was being interrogated by Gestapo official Robert Mohr on the same day, she recalled the moment when she had first seen one of the pamphlets at the university in the summer of 1942. She had asked the students standing around her what 'the White Rose' might refer to. She recalled that Hans Scholl thought he remembered something about banished aristocrats during the French

Revolution putting a white rose on their banners.[30] This might also have been behind the choice of the name.

The White Rose students drafted the pamphlets by hand, wrote them up on a Remington portable typewriter, made copies on a second-hand duplicating machine and – despite wartime shortages – obtained paper, envelopes and postage stamps in quantities small enough to be inconspicuous. Copies were posted to writers, academics, headteachers, booksellers, doctors, as well as restaurant owners, grocers and publicans in and around Munich.[31] Further copies were distributed by hand at great personal risk. According to Alexander Schmorell, they also posted copies to themselves.[32] The clandestine nature of their operations makes it difficult to say exactly how many pamphlets were made, but it is estimated that they produced around a hundred copies of each of the first four. The fact that the pamphlets had been sent by post made it much more difficult for the Gestapo to trace the perpetrators.[33]

For those who found the first White Rose pamphlet in their letterboxes in mid-June 1942, it must have been a shocking experience. The first line makes the anonymous authors' position clear and appeals to the reader's self-understanding as part of a 'civilized', or cultured, nation. The text criticizes those Germans who have passively allowed Nazism to take hold, calling them a 'spineless herd of mindless followers'.[34] It asks the reader to consider seriously the future that is to come if no one takes action, and to contemplate the consequences when 'the most horrific crimes, crimes beyond all measure, come to light'. The language of the pamphlet is forceful and urgent, referring to 'the heralds of avenging Nemesis', and likening the destruction wrought by Nazism as 'a demon that will never be sated'. The influence of Catholic intellectuals such as Muth and Haecker is palpable here.

On the night between 30 and 31 May 1942 over a thousand aircraft were dispatched in a bombing raid on the city of Cologne in the Rhineland.[35] This was the first in a series of 'thousand bomber raids', code-named 'Operation Millennium', that aimed to do as much aerial damage in the shortest time window possible. Over 3,300 buildings and 13,000 homes were destroyed.[36] Reference is made to the attack in the pamphlet, as an example of what will happen elsewhere if readers do not take action. They must 'mount passive resistance' before, 'like Cologne, the last cities are left in ruins, before the last remaining youths of this nation bleed to death in some unknown place for the sake of the hubris of a subhuman'. It is striking here that they use the term 'subhuman' (*Untermensch*), the National Socialist term for those it deemed racially inferior, to refer to Adolf Hitler.

The first pamphlet concludes with two long quotations from the great writers of German literature: one by Friedrich Schiller (1759–1805) and the other by Johann Wolfgang von Goethe (1749–1832). Schiller's text is an essay, 'The Legislation of Lycurgus and Solon' (1789), in which he contrasts oligarchic and republican forms of government.[37] The second quotation is from a relatively obscure musical drama entitled *Epimenides Awakes*

The second page of the first resistance pamphlet of the White Rose. The text includes quotations from works by Friedrich Schiller (1759–1805) and Johann Wolfgang von Goethe (1749–1832).

schreitung. Hindert eine Staatsverfassung,dass alle Kräfte, die im Menschen liegen, sich entwickeln; hindert sie die Fortschreitung des Geistes, so ist sie verwerflich und schädlich, sie mag übrigens noch so durchdacht und in ihrer Art noch so vollkommen sein. Ihre Dauerhaftigkeit selbst gereicht ihr alsdann vielmehr zum Vorwurf, als zum Ruhme - sie ist dann nur ein verlängertes Uebel; je länger sie Bestand hat, umso schädlicher ist sie.
.....Auf Unkosten aller sittlichen Gefühle wurde das politische Verdienst errungen und die Fähigkeit dazu ausgebildet. In Sparta gab es keine eheliche Liebe, keine Mutterliebe, keine kindliche Liebe, keine Freundschaft - es gab nichts als Bürger, nichts als bürgerliche Tugend.
.....Ein Staatsgesetz machte den Spartanern die Unmenschlichkeit gegen ihre Sklaven zur Pflicht; in diesen unglücklichen Schlachtopfern wurde die Menschheit beschimpft und misshandelt. In dem spartanischen Gesetzbuche selbst wurde der gefährliche Grundsatz gepredigt, Menschen als Mittel und nicht als Zwecke zu betrachten - dadurch wurden die Grundfesten des Naturrechts und der Sittlichkeit gesetzmässig eingerissen.
.....Welch schöneres Schauspiel gibt der rauhe Krieger Cajus Marcius in seinem Lager vor Rom, der Rache und Sieg aufopfert, weil er die Tränen der Mutter nicht fliessen sehen kann!"

"...Der Staat (des Lykurgus) konnte nur unter der einzigen Bedingung fortdauern, wenn der Geist des Volks stillstünde; er konnte sich also nur dadurch erhalten, dass er den höchsten und einzigen Zweck eines Staates verfehlte."

Aus Goethe "Des Epimenides Erwachen", zweiter Aufzug, vierter Auftritt:

                        Genien

                        .....
            Doch was dem Abgrund kühn entstiegen,
            Kann durch ein ehernes Geschick
            Den halben Weltkreis übersiegen,
            Zum Abgrund muss es doch zurück.
            Schon droht ein ungeheures Bangen,
            Vergebens wird er widerstehn!
            Und alle, die noch an ihn hangen,
            Sie müssen mit zu Grunde gehn

                        Hoffnung

            Nun begegn' ich meinen Braven,
            Die sich in der Nacht versammelt
            Um zu schweigen, nicht zu schlafen,
            Und das schöne Wort der Freiheit
            Wird gelispelt und gestammelt,
            Bis in ungewohnter Neuheit
            Wir an unsrer Tempel Stufen
            Wieder neu entzückt es rufen:
                 (Mit Ueberzeugung laut.)
            Freiheit!
                    (gemässigter)
                    Freiheit!
                 (von allen Seiten und Enden Echo)
                        Freiheit!
            _____

Wir bitten Sie, dieses Blatt mit möglichst vielen Durchschlägen abzuschreiben und weiter zu verteilen!

(1815), which had been referred to in one of the BBC broadcasts by the exiled author Thomas Mann in 1941.[38] The play was written for the celebrations in Berlin of Napoleon's defeat in 1813. This excerpt essentially warns that those who ally themselves with an illegitimate state will perish with it, while those who fight for freedom will flourish.[39] The quotation ends with the figure of 'Hope' repeating the word 'Freedom!' This word comes up again and again in the story of the White Rose. It recurs frequently in the pamphlets and was at the heart of their philosophical outlook. When Sophie was taken to the court from her cell on the morning of 22 February 1943, her cellmate noted that she had left behind the court's indictment on which she had written a single word: 'Freedom'. Hans Scholl's last words on the way to the guillotine were 'Long Live Freedom!'[40] Kurt Huber wrote poems for his family while he was in prison in spring 1943. In one addressed to his son, he wrote:

> I have fallen for German freedom
> Truth and honour. This trinity
> I served until my heart beat its last.[41]

The second pamphlet begins by asserting that National-al Socialism 'cannot be confronted intellectually because it is not intellectual'.[42] It has, since its inception, been based on a desire to deceive the German people. This, the pamphlet suggests, is part of Hitler's understanding of leadership. The text openly pokes fun at Hitler's political autobiography *My Struggle* (*Mein Kampf*), calling it 'a book which, despite having been written in the most appalling German that I have ever read, has been elevated to biblical status by this nation of poets and philosophers'. 'Nation of poets and philosophers' (*Land der Dichter und Denker*) is an almost proverbial phrase applied historically to Germans by themselves. In the pamphlet authors' view, that Germans have thus embraced this worthless book suggests either that they are not so gifted or that they need urgently to recover their critical faculties.

The pamphlet declares that Nazism is a 'cancerous tumour on the German people' that has grown and corrupted the whole body of the nation. Early opponents of Nazism and intellectuals hid away. But now, the authors say, the people need to work together so that everyone 'is convinced of the dire necessity of fighting against this system'. For the authors, the ends justify the means in this regard: 'An end with terror is still better than terror without end.' One of the most striking things about this pamphlet is that it explicitly denounces the persecution of European Jews, citing the 'three hundred thousand Jews' that have been murdered since the Nazi invasion of Poland. They do not mince their words here, calling this act 'the most horrific crime against human dignity, a crime unparalleled in all of human history'. The fact that the authors point to the mass murder of Jews as a reason for Germans to mount resistance makes them unique among German resistance groups.[43] They also denounce the murder of Poles, the practice of forced labour, and sending young girls into the 'brothels of the SS'.

The authors attempt to show how their fellow Germans have been taken in by Nazism and urge readers to open their eyes to the atrocities being committed in the name of the regime. Significantly, they claim that the reader *already knows* about these atrocities. Again, they refer to Nazis as 'subhumanity' (*Untermenschentum*) and call out what they see to be passivity among Germans. 'Why', they ask, 'do the German people behave so apathetically in the face of all these most atrocious, most inhumane crimes?' They assert in the most emphatic terms that Germany is burdened by 'COLLECTIVE GUILT', that everyone is 'GUILTY, GUILTY, GUILTY!' To avoid heaping more guilt upon themselves, people must *act* to overthrow Nazism. For the authors, to do so is to be viewed as a 'sacred duty'.

The quotations used at the end of the second pamphlet move from iconic writers of German literature – Goethe and Schiller – to ancient Chinese philosophy, quoting the writer and philosopher Laozi ('Master Lao' or 'Old Master'), regarded as the founding father of the philosophical system of Taoism. The text is a collection of aphorisms, and the links between the current political situation and Laozi's texts are clear: 'If a regime is unobtrusive, its people are happy. If a regime is oppressive, the people are broken.' The German translation of Laozi which the White Rose used contains the word 'Reich', meaning 'empire', which for the student authors in the Third Reich had a particularly direct resonance.[44]

The third pamphlet begins with a slight misquotation from Cicero (106–43 BCE): 'Salus publica suprema lex' (The welfare of the people is the supreme law), from *De legibus* (*On the Laws*), which explores ideas around natural law and constitutional reform. The White Rose pamphlet begins with a discussion of ideal forms of state. It cites Augustine of Hippo's *The City of God against the*

Pagans (*c.*426 CE) here, a foundational text of Western thought, which explores suffering, evil, free will and original sin. They write that, while they do not want to discuss the merits or failings of all possible forms of government, they want to make clear that 'every single person is entitled to a viable and just government that ensures the freedom of the individual as well as the welfare of society as a whole.'[45] Germany, however, is a 'dictatorship of evil'. Again, the authors criticize readers' passivity: 'If you know that, then why don't you act?' It is a 'MORAL DUTY' to overthrow the system, and time is running out.

The authors address the fact that readers may not know *how* to act, precisely *how* to overthrow National Socialism. This, they argue, will not be possible through 'individualistic opposition' but through 'the conviction and energy of people acting together'. Every reader must engage in 'PASSIVE RESISTANCE' to bring down National Socialism and to bring an end to the war. Victory for Germany would, they argue, 'have dreadful, unimaginable consequences'. They advocate sabotage – of factories, Nazi events, universities, cultural events, the arts and the media. They even warn against giving to charity street collections undertaken on behalf of the war effort, because this will only continue to benefit and support the state. They signal that they intend to write further pamphlets to explain their views in more detail. The pamphlet ends with an excerpt from *Politics* by the Greek philosopher Aristotle (384–322 BCE). This is a fundamental work of political philosophy that asks how it might be possible to preserve a good society in dangerous times. The extract used in the pamphlet focuses on tyranny: a system that means that citizens are spied on, come to suspect and distrust one another and are bled dry financially. The final line of the quotation is the most apt in the context of the early 1940s: 'And the tyrant also has a constant inclination to provoke war.'

The fourth pamphlet begins with a play on two German proverbs: 'He who will not hear, must feel' and 'The burnt child dreads the fire'.[46] 'There is an old and wise saying, which we preach to children time and again, that "he who will not listen, must feel". However, clever children will burn their fingers on a hot stove only once.'[47] Here, the pamphlet suggests that what is easily learned by children seems incomprehensible to the adult German population. The text makes reference to recent Nazi victories in Africa and Russia, and the unsuccessful German offensive in Egypt when they failed to break through the British lines. There is, the pamphlet states, no reason to be optimistic about the continuing advance into Russia because of the human cost it entails. The male students of the White Rose knew this only too well from their own experiences on the front lines in France and Russia. It is unsurprising, then, that the imagery they evoke is so stark here: 'It is harvest time, and the Reaper cuts into the ripe crop with broad strokes. Grief settles into the country's cottages, and no one is there to dry the mothers' tears.'

Again, this pamphlet explicitly attacks Adolf Hitler, though this time it is more direct than the mockery of the second pamphlet. Hitler is denounced as a liar who commits blasphemy by speaking of God when, the authors state, he really means 'the power of the Evil One, of the fallen angel, of Satan'. The White Rose circle was influenced by, and drew inspiration from, a number of individuals, among them Theodor Haecker, an authority on the works of the Danish philosopher Søren Kierkegaard, and translator from English into German of some of the philosophical and theological works of John Henry Newman.[48] Under the Nazis, Haecker was banned from speaking publicly or publishing any writings, whether his own or translations of others. He kept a secret diary documenting his internal resistance to the regime, which his teenage daughter smuggled out of their flat when it was searched by the Gestapo following the first White Rose trial.[49] Haecker's influence is discernible here in the fourth pamphlet, which draws on theology and metaphysics, presenting Hitler himself as the Antichrist.[50] Only with God, the pamphlet claims, can he be overcome.

Again, the text appeals to readers *as Christians* and demands they take a stand. It ends with two quotations underlining the arguments of the main text. The first is a short extract from the Old Testament book of Ecclesiastes that explores the essential question about the purpose of life. The quotation used by the White Rose draws attention to those who are oppressed and have 'no comforter'. The second quotation is by the eighteenth-century German Romantic Georg Philipp Friedrich Freiherr von Hardenberg (1772–1801), who wrote under the pen-name Novalis. In his essay 'Christendom or Europe' (1799), written in the light of the French Revolution, which in his view was chaotic and irreligious, Novalis explored the possibility of a new Europe. He wrote, as the White Rose quoted, that 'True anarchy is the generative element of religion.' Here, the White Rose pamphlet emphasizes Germany's suffering in the war, but also the hope that would come when it could build a new world. The fourth pamphlet ends with an assurance that the White Rose is not in the pay of a foreign power, for the first time referring to the resistance group specifically. The pamphlet ends with a bold declaration, one that has become most frequently associated with the White Rose: 'We will not be silent. We are your bad conscience. The White Rose will never leave you in peace!'

One of the most striking things about the first four pamphlets is the use of quotations from other sources. These draw on a wide range of philosophical ideas and influences, from totemic German writers such as Goethe, Schiller and Novalis, as well as Aristotle, the Old Testament and ancient Chinese philosophy. The body of thought from which the White Rose authors drew and which they offered in part as validation of their own position, expresses well their rich and diverse cultural backgrounds and interests. The quotations are intellectually and culturally 'demanding'.[51] Wolfgang Huber, the son of Professor Kurt Huber, has suggested that the organization of the quotations has its own internal logic: the pamphlets begin with poetry (Goethe and Schiller), then they move to philosophy (Laozi and Aristotle), and finally move into the realm of Christianity (the Old Testament and Novalis). In this way they reach a kind of highpoint of intensity.[52] They become increasingly urgent and serious. The pamphlets were undoubtedly the result of the authors' 'moral and ethical outrage', but they were also political texts,[53] making reference to current events and demonstrating a historical understanding of political systems. The pamphlets made an appeal to the educated and intellectual middle class, as members of the cultured German nation and as Christians. They exhorted readers to reflect critically on the hegemony of Nazism and appealed to them as fellow Germans. They suggest to readers that they, the people of Germany, are, as it were, *better* than what they have become under Nazism. As they would go on to declare in the fifth pamphlet: 'Act — prove that you think differently!'[54]

Traute Lafrenz recalled that when she first read the pamphlets, she had a strong sense that they must be by members of her own circle, and then came to believe that Hans Scholl must be behind them.[55] Inge Scholl recounted a story about Sophie Scholl's first encounter with the pamphlets. Sophie had been at university for about six weeks when she caught sight of the first pamphlet. By chance, when waiting for her brother Hans Scholl in his rooms not long after, she happened to flick through his books, and found a passage in a book by Schiller that had been marked. It was the same passage that had been in the White Rose pamphlet. She is reported to have confronted her brother and at this point became involved in the White Rose activities.[56]

What was it that led the members of the White Rose to embark on this decisive and highly risky endeavour, and at this particular time? From their own statements made later under interrogation, from the letters they wrote around this time, and from what we know of their activities and the circles in which they moved, it seems

clear that the decision to act was the result of an intensi-
fication of their own private opposition to the state, and a
sense of the urgent need to act, fuelled by discourse and
dialogue with others. The pamphlets were a provocation
to German readers to recognize the damage being done
to the nation and its people by Nazism, and to acknowledge their own complicity in that process. The authors
express concern both for 'their own' people, namely those
not directly targeted by the state, but confined within in
its structures and institutions, and demand compassion
and action on behalf of direct victims of Nazi oppression. In this way the White Rose advocated for others
who lacked their advantages, and exhorted others to do
likewise. They certainly engage with intellectual arguments, but they also appeal to conscience.

THE RUSSIAN FRONT, JULY–NOVEMBER 1942

The fourth pamphlet was completed and distributed in
July 1942. Later that month, on the 23rd, Hans Scholl,
Alexander Schmorell and Willi Graf left Munich for a
three-month tour of duty at the Russian front.[57] Sophie
and Christoph went to Munich East Station (*Ostbahnhof*)
to see them off. Willi, who had not long returned from an
extended period of deployment in Russia,[58] recorded the
event in his diary:

> At the station by 7 a.m. Loading. Didn't set off until
> 11. Our compartment is good. I feel at ease, we have
> space to ourselves and can talk. That's something to
> be grateful for. Passed Regensburg, the Danube. It is a
> nice afternoon.[59]

On 23 July 1942 at the *Ostbahnhof* station in Munich, Sophie Scholl bids farewell to her brother Hans Scholl (*left*), Alexander Schmorell (*far right*), and their friends as they leave for the Eastern Front.

The journey took them through Warsaw, where they witnessed the clearing of the Jewish ghetto. They saw starving men, women and children on the way to the station where they were to be deported, to Auschwitz, Treblinka, Majdanek and Sobibor.[60] Willi Graf commented in his diary: 'Midday in Warsaw. It's very hot.... In the late afternoon we go into town. Misery looks us in the eye. We turn away.'[61] In a letter to his parents the following day, Hans Scholl commented on the same scene:

> After a long journey through Germany and Poland, we have arrived. The journey itself was pleasant. I occupied a whole compartment with my friends, and when we weren't sleeping we passed the time with meaningful conversation and games, and frequently we would stare

for hours on end out of the window at the countryside going by. In particular, we were mesmerized by the unending plain of the East. ... It would sicken me to stay in Warsaw any longer. Thank God we go tomorrow.[62]

On 1 August they arrived at the town of Vyazma, and from there they travelled on to Gzhatsk, where they were to be stationed, just 6 miles from the front line.[63] Hans wrote to Kurt Huber on behalf of himself and some of the others:

After a long and varied journey, we arrived in a small, virtually obliterated town east of Vyazma two weeks ago. We spend our days here doing nothing. ... I am in a company with three good friends, whom you know. My Russian friend [Alexander Schmorell] is especially useful. I am also making great efforts to learn the Russian language. We go and see the Russians in the evening and drink schnapps with them and sing.[64]

These three months in Russia proved profoundly important for all three of the White Rose students. They saw the suffering of the Polish inhabitants of Warsaw, spent time drinking, singing and communicating with Russian people. For Alexander Schmorell, born to a Russian mother and who spoke Russian fluently, this was a return to his longed-for homeland. Their experiences in Russia provided further proof of the lie that was the Nazi assertion that Russians were innately inferior to Germans. This was achieved through encounters with ordinary people and through a deep sense of a shared literary culture throughout Russian society.

It was also a time for discussion and philosophical reflection. Like Willi Graf, Hans Scholl kept a diary during this period. On 7 August 1942 he wrote of the monotony of life at the front and his struggle to make sense of it:

I am tired from doing nothing. And the bunker is shaking and groaning since the Russians are firing bomb after bomb at the landing strip. I am surplus to requirements here. I am a lone wanderer in the middle of some sensical nonsense. The war has me in its thrall only between the firing and explosion of artillery shells.[65]

In August, Hans Scholl's father, Robert Scholl, was arrested and sentenced to a four-month prison sentence after his secretary denounced him for defaming Hitler.[66] He had called him a 'scourge of God'. Hans Scholl reflected on his father's incarceration:

My father is sitting in prison. He is almost certainly thinking about me right now. I'm sitting on a wooden crate. A candle is flickering as it burns, strange figures melting down its side, little wax bodies formed by chance, or by fate for all I care. The candle will get smaller and smaller until it eventually goes out. What is death? Why are people so afraid of it? Why do your fingers tremble when you touch a dead body? And then, not without a hint of lust, you think about a mother's tears, or a lover's heart which is in such pain that it wants to stop beating altogether, and then a thought creeps into your head, just a thought, which you just so happen to let linger – completely secretly, of course that *you* are still alive, that *your* heart is still beating, and that death actually concerns you about as much as the corns on your neighbour's feet. My father in prison. Explosions outside. Bombs.[67]

During this period Christoph Probst, who was in a different military company, felt the loss of his like-minded comrades. He wrote to Hans Scholl in October 1942:

It's funny that I've just received your first letter since you left, because in the last week such a strong feeling of longing for you all has awoken in me. It is true – I have experienced & seen everything as if we were all together & have often found our separation so very painful.[68]

Hans Scholl, Willi Graf and Alexander Schmorell left the front on 30 October and arrived back in Munich a week later. On 7 November Sophie Scholl wrote to Fritz Hartnagel, a young officer in the Luftwaffe whom she had met at a dance in 1937. The two had maintained a close, romantic friendship throughout this period, writing regularly and meeting when they could, which was increasingly infrequently after the outbreak of war. She wrote:

Hans is coming back from Russia tonight. I suppose I should be pleased that he's back with us again, and I am, I'm already imagining the days we'll spend together in Munich in our little flat, days that could well be productive. But I can't truly be happy. The constant uncertainty that we live in nowadays prevents us from making nice plans for the next day and casts a shadow over all the days yet to come, it weighs me down night and day and doesn't give me a minute's rest. When will the time finally come when we won't have to focus all our strength and all our attention on things that aren't worth lifting a finger for? Every word is scrutinized before it's even spoken, in case there is even a hint of ambiguity about it. Our trust in other people has to give way to mistrust and caution. Oh, how tiring and sometimes disheartening it is. But no, I won't let anything take away my courage, these trivial things will not get the better of me, when I know there are other joys that surpass them. When I think of this, my strength returns, and I want to cry out a word of encouragement to everyone else who is oppressed.[69]

The next phase of the White Rose resistance was about to begin.

JANUARY–FEBRUARY 1943: PAMPHLETS V AND VI

When Hans Scholl, Alexander Schmorell and Willi Graf returned to Germany in November 1942 the group resumed the pamphlet campaign. In November, Hans Scholl and Alexander Schmorell travelled to Stuttgart to meet with Eugen Grimminger (1892–1986), a friend of Robert Scholl's and an opponent of Nazism. They apprised him of the resistance activities, and he offered his support, including money and contacts.[70] In December 1942 Hans Scholl told Kurt Huber about the pamphlet campaign and at this point he became actively involved.[71] That same month Christoph Probst was transferred to a student company in Innsbruck, though he managed to travel back and forth to Munich to participate in the resistance activities. By January 1943 Willi Graf, Hans Scholl, Alexander Schmorell and Sophie Scholl had all resumed their studies in Munich after the vacation. On 13 January Willi Graf noted in his diary: 'Visited Hans. Still there by the evening. We're really getting started with the work, the ball is starting to roll.'[72]

Between 14 and 24 January, Franklin D. Roosevelt, Winston Churchill and other Allied leaders met at the Casablanca Conference, the result of which was a declaration demanding Germany's unconditional surrender. The fifth pamphlet of the White Rose appeared some time between 27 and 29 January,[73] and by 18 February copies had reached Munich, Augsburg, Salzburg, Vienna, Linz, Stuttgart and Frankfurt am Main.[74] There is a marked difference between the first four pamphlets and the fifth. To begin with, it looks different on the page: there is more space between the lines, it is shorter, and the title is no longer the 'Pamphlets of the White Rose', but rather 'Pamphlets of the Resistance Movement in Germany – AN APPEAL TO ALL GERMANS!'[75] There is a more liberal use of emphasis through exclamation marks and spacing. There are no quotations from other sources. The language is 'clearer' and 'more political',[76] and there is an even greater sense of urgency. As Christiane Moll has pointed out, it is the pamphlet most heavily influenced by British propaganda.[77] The text was written by Hans Scholl and edited principally by Kurt Huber.[78]

The pamphlet begins by asserting that the war is almost over, and that Hitler is leading Germany to ruin. Again, the authors call out their readers' passivity and wilful ignorance. The pamphlet again explicitly mentions Jewish persecution that had been the subject of British propaganda reports in December 1942. The authors ask: 'Germans! Do you and your children want to suffer the same fate that befell the Jews?' Again, the openness with which the mass murder of Jews is discussed here is remarkable. It is also striking that the pamphlet focuses on what will happen *after* the war, how Germany will be seen by the rest of the world in the years to come: 'Shall we be forever hated and shunned by the whole world? No! So separate yourselves from the subhuman nature of National Socialism!' Once again, the authors take the pejorative word the Nazis used to refer to Jews and other persecuted groups, 'subhumans' (*Untermenschen*), and apply it to the Nazis themselves. It is National Socialism, and not Bolshevism, that Germans should fear, they claim.

In the final section the pamphlet suggests what might go in place of the corrupt system it aims to overthrow. This would be founded through 'the generous collaboration of the European nations' and must be 'federalist'; that is, it must not be dominated by 'Prussian militarism'. The pamphlet ends with a utopian vision: 'Freedom of speech, freedom of faith, protection of the individual citizen from the despotism of criminal and violent states: these are the foundations of the new Europe.'

On 3 February news arrived of the German army's defeat at Stalingrad. While the original pamphlet campaign had been precipitated by a shared desire for change, the suffering of Germans at Hitler's hands was a decisive moment prompting immediate action. That same night Alexander Schmorell, Hans Scholl and Willi Graf graffitied buildings in the centre of Munich and around the university.[79] They painted the slogans 'DOWN WITH HITLER' and 'FREEDOM'. On 8 February the theatre director Falk Harnack (1913–1991) came to Munich and made contact with the White Rose through their mutual friend Lilo Fürst-Ramdohr (1913–2013).[80] Harnack was the brother of Arvid Harnack, a leading figure in the Red Orchestra (*Rote Kapelle*) resistance circle. After meeting with Hans Scholl, Alexander Schmorell, Willi Graf and Kurt Huber Harnack returned to Berlin, where he agreed to meet Hans Scholl on the evening of 25 February. That afternoon, Harnack visited the brothers Dietrich Bonhoeffer (1906–1945) and Klaus Bonhoeffer (1901–1945), who were also active in the resistance within Germany. It was intended that the four should meet later that day when Hans Scholl arrived in Berlin.[81] Falk Harnack waited for him in vain, unaware that he had already been put to death.

Following the news of Stalingrad, Kurt Huber wrote the text of the sixth pamphlet at Hans Scholl's request. He even asked him to write it in the voice of a student, and indeed the heading of the pamphlet simply reads: 'Fellow students!' Huber had edited Hans Scholl's writing in the fifth pamphlet, and now the students did the same to their academic mentor. While they were in agreement with what Huber had written, Alexander Schmorell and Hans Scholl vehemently opposed one passage:

> Students. You have put yourselves entirely at the disposal of the German Wehrmacht on the front line, in the barracks, in the face of the enemy, in attending to the wounded, but also in the laboratory and at work. There can be no other goal for us all than the destruction of Russian Bolshevism in all its forms. Stand firm with the ranks of our glorious Wehrmacht.[82]

For Alexander Schmorell and Hans Scholl, who had served at the front, this was an unacceptable portrayal of the Wehrmacht's role in the war. There was a heated debate, cross words, and Huber left. Kurt Huber never saw Hans Scholl again after that meeting. The next time he would see Alexander Schmorell would be at their trial two months later.

The sixth pamphlet is noticeably shorter than the other texts, taking up just one side of paper instead of two (see p. 118). From the very beginning the pamphlet lays the blame for Stalingrad squarely at Hitler's door, and with biting sarcasm it declares: 'Führer we thank you', using a phrase common at Nazi rallies and in propaganda.[83] Again, this pamphlet emphasizes the urgent need to act and to bring an end to the death and destruction wrought by the war: 'The day of reckoning has come'. Students need to see that they have been the victims of 'Ideological Education' in the Hitler Youth, the Sturmabteilung (SA), the Schutzstaffel (SS), and elite schools designed to train future leaders (*Ordensburgen*). The Nazis have used these to stifle independent thought and create mindless followers.

The pamphlet also makes reference to an event that had taken place at the university in Munich a month earlier. On 13 January Paul Giesler, the regional governor (*Gauleiter*) of Bavaria, had given a speech to mark the 470th anniversary of the foundation of the University, in which he upbraided female students for studying and thereby shirking their duties, declaring that 'the natural place for a woman is not at the university, but with her family, at the side of her husband'.[84] He later offered to find husbands for any women who were 'not pretty enough' to do so by themselves.[85] A protest ensued. One student, Marie-Luise Jahn (1918–2010) – who would later come to be involved in the White Rose resistance herself – recalled that for those who were opposed to the state the Munich students' reaction was 'wonderful' and might be a sign that further opposition would follow.[86] However, this turned out not to be the case. Such protest as there was proved to be short-lived. Kurt Huber was reportedly incensed by the incident and resolved to write a pamphlet in response.[87] The pamphlet he wrote lauds the 'dignified response' of women studying at the university in the face of 'lewd jokes' and Giesler's 'insult' to their honour.

The pamphlet appeals to students to act, again pointing out the 'duty' of the individual to take action to shape the future. It argues that the notions of 'freedom' and 'honour' have been corrupted by the Nazis. Only if the young people of Germany take action will the nation be able to be born anew after the war ends. The pamphlet dispenses with the closing plea to make and distribute further copies. Instead, it calls on students to rise up and participate in the shaping of Germany's future.

While this pamphlet also dispenses with long quotations from other sources, as the previous one had done, it does include a line from a patriotic poem, 'Soldier's Song', written by the poet and soldier Theodor Körner (1791–1813): 'Rise up, my people, the beacons are aflame!' The text makes reference to the German Campaign of 1813 when Napoleon was decisively defeated at the Battle of Leipzig. It is this, the pamphlet declares, that will enable Germany to 'break the terror' of National Socialism now, over two centuries later. It is ironic that the propaganda minister Joseph Goebbels, in his speech exhorting Germans to accept 'total war' on 18 February, would use a similar call to his audience, also quoting the soldier-poet Theodor Körner: 'People, rise up, and storm, break loose!'[88] The contents of the sixth pamphlet were apparently so shocking that when it was read aloud at the second White Rose trial in April 1943, Kurt Huber's defence lawyer refused to represent him, and he was left to mount his own defence.[89] Huber insisted that the pamphlet did not contain anything that was not true, and that he would not retract a single word of it. 'History,' he declared, 'will affirm Hitler's full responsibility for Stalingrad.'[90]

On 12 February Hans Scholl and Alexander Schmorell begin to distribute the sixth pamphlet.[91] The group had printed around 3,000 copies,[92] of which between 800 and 1,200 were sent out in the post.[93] On the night of 15 February they distributed further copies around Munich as well as repeating the graffiti operation with Willi Graf they had undertaken earlier that month. Sophie Scholl and Willi Graf also distributed the pamphlets at great personal risk. The Gestapo had been aware of the White Rose pamphlets since they were first produced in the summer of 1942, not least because recipients had done as the law required and had handed them in to their NSDAP building warden (*Blockwart*) or local Gestapo headquarters. In January 1943 a special commission was established to investigate the pamphlets, led by Gestapo official Robert Mohr (1897–1977).[94] In mid-February 1943, a professor at the University of Munich, Richard Harder (1896–1957), was commissioned to analyse the pamphlets with a view to better identifying the authors. In his report, Harder noted that the pamphlets were written in an excellent style of German and that the authors must be intellectuals who had made a sustained and detailed study of German literature, as well as possessing other academic qualities,[95] though he considered the name 'The White Rose' rather 'kitsch'.[96] Harder concluded that, given the language and references used, the pamphlets 'will not (and cannot) meet with a positive response among soldiers and workers'.[97]

'AND WHEN YOU HAVE CHOSEN, ACT': CHRISTOPH PROBST'S DRAFT PAMPHLET

When Hans Scholl and his sister were arrested on 18 February he had in his pocket the handwritten draft of a pamphlet that Christoph Probst had written a month earlier at his request.[98] The text began with one word: 'Stalingrad!' Probst described the German defeat, denouncing the fact that thousands of German soldiers had been abandoned by their superior officers and left to die senselessly on the battlefield. This catastrophic defeat was juxtaposed with the unconditional surrender of Tripoli to the Allied forces on 23 January, after which the victors let citizens' lives continue as normal. Roosevelt was referred to as 'the most powerful man in the world' and Hitler as a mass murderer and 'military fraudster'. The pamphlet closed with an ultimatum: 'Hitler and his regime must fall so that Germany may live on. The choice is yours: Stalingrad and ruin, or Tripoli and hope for the future. And when you have chosen, act.'[99]

When he was apprehended, Hans Scholl attempted to get rid of the draft that would have incriminated his friend, but he was unable to do so and the arresting officers discovered it. The handwriting was later compared with letters from Christoph Probst to Hans Scholl found during a search of the Scholls' Munich flat. As soon as he was identified as the author of the pamphlet, Christoph Probst's fate was sealed. He was arrested on Saturday, 20 February at his barracks in Innsbruck as he was picking up a leave permit. His wife, Herta Probst, was unwell following the birth of their third child on 21 January, and he was planning to visit them. As he wrote to his sister Angelika Probst from prison: 'On Saturday, as I was on my way to pick up my leave permit for Tegernsee, I was arrested and taken to Munich. Now I am in a cell for the first time in my life and I do not know what the next day holds for me.'[100]

The torn scraps of the draft pamphlet were pieced together by the Gestapo. During his interrogation on Sunday 21 February Christoph Probst was forced to fill in the gaps where they had been unable to decipher the text.[101] The pamphlet was never finished, never printed, and never distributed. After the war, it was only uncovered when, in the early 1990s, the complete set of files pertaining to the first White Rose trial, thought lost or destroyed, were located in the former National Socialist archives that had been housed in the archive of the Ministry for State Security (*Stasi*) in East Germany.[102]

THE FIRST TRIAL

The first White Rose trial began on the morning of
Monday, 22 February 1943 in the Palace of Justice in
Munich. The People's Court (*Volksgerichtshof*) was
presided over by judge Roland Freisler (1893–1945),
who had been dispatched from Berlin. Freisler had
been an ardent supporter of Nazism from its early
days. Known as 'raving Roland', he was infamous for
his vehemence and ruthlessness on the bench.[103] A
law student in Munich, Leo Samberger (1913–1993),
recalled attending the trial, which was to all intents
and purposes a show trial. Freisler conducted it 'with
the utmost severity',[104] while the three defendants
were 'calm, collected, clear and brave' in the face of his
aggressive questioning.[105]

Earlier that weekend, Traute Lafrenz had travelled to
Ulm to inform the family of the Scholl siblings' arrest.
On Sunday, 21 February an anonymous call from a student in Munich informed the parents that their children
would be tried the following day. Robert and Magdalena
Scholl travelled from Ulm and managed to enter the
courtroom as the verdicts were being read out. Their
other son, Werner Scholl, had also managed to get into
the courtroom. By 1 p.m. the trial was over. The sentence
of the court declared that the accused had 'called for
the sabotage of the war effort and armaments and for
the overthrow of the National Socialist way of life of our
people', had 'most vulgarly defamed the Führer' and so
aided Germany's enemies and weakened national security.[106] Hans Scholl, Sophie Scholl and Christoph Probst
were taken to Stadelheim Prison in the southern part of

the city, where Hitler himself has served a sentence of four weeks back in 1922.[107]

Robert and Magdalena Scholl were able to see their children briefly in the prison. An hour before their execution, Hans Scholl and Sophie Scholl were both visited by the prison's Protestant chaplain, the Revd Dr Karl Alt (1897–1951), who gave them Communion and prayed with them. Christoph Probst requested the Catholic chaplain, Father Heinrich Sperr (1909–1964), and received the sacraments of baptism and the Eucharist.[108] At 5 p.m. the three were executed by guillotine. Sophie Scholl was taken first, then Hans Scholl, then Christoph Probst. The whole process lasted less than ten minutes.

THE AFTERSHOCKS OF THE FIRST TRIAL

The day after Sophie Scholl, Hans Scholl and Christoph Probst were executed, there was a notice in a Munich newspaper reporting that three 'despicable criminals' had been disposed of.[109] On the morning of Tuesday, 23 February Sophie and Hans Scholl's mother, Magdalena Scholl, wrote to Fritz Hartnagel to ask him to make an appeal for clemency for her children. His status as an officer would have carried weight with the authorities. What Magdalena Scholl could not have known, however, when she and her husband left the prison the previous day, was that her children were to be executed that same afternoon.[110] It was usual for at least a period of ninety-nine days to elapse between a sentence being passed and an execution carried out.[111] However, Berlin was demanding a swift end to the matter. Fritz Hartnagel had been deployed as part of the invasion of Russia in May 1942, and in November was among the 300,000 German troops surrounded by the Red Army in Stalingrad. He was airlifted out on 22 January 1943 and sent to a military hospital in Lemberg (now Lviv, Ukraine) where he was treated for frostbite and had to have two fingers amputated. On 22 February he wrote to Sophie from the hospital, unaware that, by the evening, she was no longer alive. He thanked her for writing to him, regretted that his own letters did not seem to have been reaching her, and asked how she was getting on:

> Your letters do me so much good. ... And when I hold your letter in my hands, and as the first rays of sunshine stream in through the window, I'm filled with the warmth of spring. Or at least a sense that spring is on its way and a fervent hope that it will soon be here. ... But for now you must tell me more about where you are, I still know nothing about it. For instance, is Hans still with you in Munich? And who else is there?
>
> I spend many hours of the day with you. Take this as proof.[112]

When he received Magdalena Scholl's first letter at the end of February, or in early March, Fritz Hartnagel set off for Berlin to plead for clemency. On Saturday, 27 February he sent a telegram to the office of the People's Court in Berlin, requesting a delay to the enforcement of Sophie and Hans's execution so that he could submit an appeal for clemency.[113] It was only when he telephoned the Scholls' house in Ulm and spoke to Werner Scholl that he learned the three were no longer alive.[114] In late

February 1943 Christoph Probst's wife Herta was in hospital with childbed fever, following the birth of their daughter a month earlier. On 22 February, the day of the trial, she was visited by Traute Lafrenz and Werner Scholl, who told her that her husband had been sentenced to death. She sent a telegram to the Munich director of public prosecutions (*Generalstaatsanwalt*) pleading for clemency.[115] Robert and Magdalena Scholl also submitted a plea for clemency for the three prisoners, but it was in vain. Herta found out on Tuesday 23 February that her husband had already been executed. She had had no idea that he was involved in the resistance.[116]

Christoph Probst wrote to her from prison on the day of his execution, playing down the seriousness of what lay ahead:

> Following an unfortunate series of events, I have ended up at the Gestapo in Munich. But I am not doing badly here at all. I feel quite calm and await the things that are to come. Never have I drawn so much strength from my love for you as I do now.[117]

It perhaps seems strange that a man with a wife and three young children should have taken such risks, knowing what the outcome could be. The journalist and historian Miriam Gebhardt has suggested that he did it not in spite of, but *because of* the children.[118] He wanted a better future for them and acted accordingly.

On the evening of Wednesday, 24 February Hans Scholl, Sophie Scholl and Christoph Probst were buried in the Munich Cemetery at Perlacher Forst, directly opposite Stadelheim Prison where they had been executed.

The funeral was overseen by Gestapo agents hoping to identify other members of the group. Of their friends, only Traute Lafrenz attended.[119] Magdalena Scholl wrote again to Fritz Hartnagel: 'Yesterday before sundown we laid our two children to rest.... We will not let ourselves be ashamed of Sofie. The chaplain said he had never seen such courage.'[120]

As his friends were being buried, Alexander Schmorell was arrested following a complicated and daring escape attempt that had begun after the Scholl siblings were apprehended. Following the Scholls' arrest on 18 February, the Schmorells' home was searched. On Saturday 20 February, equipped with a false passport and provisions, Alexander Schmorell left Munich in the hope of escaping to the East.[121] Meanwhile a warrant was issued for his arrest, and a photograph and description of him were circulated on the front page of a Munich newspaper on 24 February, along with the promise of a 1,000 Reichsmark reward for his capture.[122] His escape plans having failed, he returned to Munich on 24 February. He was on his way to find shelter with an old girlfriend in the Schwabing district when the air-raid siren sounded. He entered a shelter, only to be recognized. He did not know that he had become a wanted man. He was apprehended at around 10.30 p.m. and taken to the Gestapo prison in the Wittelsbach Palace, where Willi Graf was still in custody.[123]

On Saturday, 27 February Kurt Huber was at his home in the Gräfeling suburb of Munich along with his 13-year-old daughter Birgit. His wife, Clara Huber, was away visiting, and his 4-year-old son Wolfgang ('Wolfi') was with his maternal grandmother in Uffing am Staffel-see, 40 miles south of Munich. At 6.30 a.m. the Gestapo arrived at the door, the house was searched and Kurt Huber was arrested. As her father was led away, Birgit Huber told him, 'Don't be home late!'[124] In the days that followed, several others associated with the White Rose were arrested and interrogated, and on 19 April 1943 the second White Rose trial took place at the Munich Palace of Justice. Once again, the judge Roland Freisler was dispatched from Berlin to preside. The trial began at 9 o'clock in the morning and lasted over twelve hours.[125] The principal defendants were Alexander Schmorell, Willi Graf and Kurt Huber, all of whom received the death sentence. Their crimes were that they had 'incited sabotage of military arms and the overthrow of the National Socialist way of life' through their pamphlets, had 'promoted defeatist ideas', had 'insulted the name of the Führer in the basest way possible and in this way aided and abetted the enemy of the Reich', and had 'undermined' Germany's military strength.[126]

There were eleven other defendants at the trial: Traute Lafrenz, Gisela Schertling and Katharina Schüddekopf, received prison sentences of a year each; Heinrich Guter got eighteen months, Susanne Hirzel six months, her brother Hans Hirzel and Franz Josef Müller five years, Heinz Bollinger and Helmut Bauer 7 years, and Eugen Grimminger ten years.[127] Falk Harnack was surprisingly acquitted, though this turned out to be a Gestapo ploy to get him to lead them to information about the Red Orchestra resistance group, in which his brother and sister-in-law had been leading figures.

Alexander Schmorell and Kurt Huber were executed on 13 July 1943. Willi Graf was executed on 12 October 1943. Still further trials followed. On 13 July 1943 the bookshop owner Josef Söhngen received a six-month prison sentence for providing his bookshop as a hiding place;[128] the artist Wilhelm Geyer, the architect Manfred Eickemeyer and Harald Dohrn (Christoph Probst's father-in-law) were acquitted through lack of evidence.[129] On 3 April Willi Bollinger, a friend of Willi Graf who had distributed copies of the fifth pamphlet in Saarbrücken, as well as providing assistance to the group, received a three-month prison sentence for failing to report an act of treason.

Retribution for the 'crimes' committed by the core White Rose members did not end with their executions. Their families endured 'kin liability' or 'family liability punishment' (*Sippenhaft*), a practice in which a family was punished for the crimes of one of its members. Anneliese Graf had been arrested at the same time as her brother Willi, and Christoph Probst's sister Angelika was also arrested. The two ended up in the same cell.[130] Clara Huber was taken into custody on 3 March, as were her two sisters-in-law.[131] The Scholls' parents and two sisters, Elisabeth and Inge, were also arrested.[132] The other Scholl sibling, Werner, was spared as he was due to return to the front. He returned to Russia and in June 1944 was listed as missing in action. Alexander Schmorell's father, Erich, and his stepmother, Elisabeth, were also both taken into Gestapo custody in February and then again in April 1943.[133] In some cases, several months elapsed before family members were released, despite their protestations that they had known nothing of the White Rose resistance activities.[134]

'AND YET THEIR SPIRIT LIVES ON!'
THE PAMPHLET CAMPAIGN CONTINUED

Even after the six members of the core group had been imprisoned, and almost all of them executed, the pamphlet campaign continued. Two students, Hans Leipelt and Marie-Luise Jahn, made copies of the sixth pamphlet and distributed them in Hamburg. To the copies of the pamphlet they made, they added the phrase 'And yet their spirit lives on!' They also collected money for Kurt Huber's widow Clara, who, left virtually destitute after her husband's execution, had been issued with a bill for 'wear and tear to the guillotine'.[135] Marie-Luise Jahn, Hans Leipelt and others were arrested in October 1943. A year elapsed before they were tried by the People's Court in Donauwörth in southern Germany on 13 October 1944. Jahn received a twelve-year prison sentence; Leipelt was sentenced to death and executed at Stadelheim Prison in Munich on 29 January 1945. Three months later, Christoph Probst's father-in-law, Harald Dohrn, was one of a number of individuals executed for their support of the resistance group Action for the Freedom of Bavaria (Freiheitsaktion Bayern) that in the last throes of the war sought to overthrow Nazism and establish an interim government. He was shot in the woods at Perlacher Forst, not far from where his son-in-law and the Scholl siblings were buried.[136] Further copies of the sixth pamphlet were distributed in Berlin by a resistance circle known as 'Uncle Emil', and copies appeared in Munich in the summer of 1944 under the heading 'Free Student Body Munich'.[137]

In mid-August 1943 Clara Huber was called into the Gestapo offices in Munich and told that the Allies had dropped thousands of pamphlets across Germany.[138] She was astonished. It turned out that Kurt Huber's pamphlet had been smuggled out of Germany by Helmuth James Graf von Moltke (1907–1945), a leading figure in the Kreisau Circle (Kreisauer Kreis), a group of German dissidents who opposed Adolf Hitler and Nazism. Von Moltke had taken the pamphlet from Munich to Berlin and then to Norway, where it was translated and published by a Norwegian resistance group. It then went via Sweden to England. The British Political Warfare Executive reproduced the pamphlet with a new title: 'A German Pamphlet: Manifesto of the Munich Students'. As the families of those who had already been executed were mourning their dead, and Willi Graf was still being held in a prison cell in Munich, millions of copies had been dropped by the RAF over northern and central Germany.

A new introduction prefaced the pamphlet, explaining that it represented the views of many students, but more than that – of Germans in all walks of life who had 'recognized the truth of Germany's situation'.[139] The Allies, it claimed, were going to win the war. It presented the German reader with a stark challenge: 'we do not see why rational and respectable people in Germany should

A copy of the sixth White Rose pamphlet printed and distributed by the British Warfare Executive in 1943. The word *Feindpropaganda* (enemy propaganda) has been written in blue pencil across the page.

EIN DEUTSCHES FLUGBLATT

DIES ist der Text eines deutschen Flugblatts, von dem ein Exemplar nach England gelangt ist. Studenten der Universität München haben es im Februar dieses Jahres verfasst und in der Universität verteilt. Sechs von ihnen sind dafür hingerichtet worden, andere wurden eingesperrt, andere strafweise an die Front geschickt. Seither werden auch an allen anderen deutschen Universitäten die Studenten „ausgesiebt". Das Flugblatt drückt also offenbar die Gesinnungen eines beträchtlichen Teils der deutschen Studenten aus.

Aber es sind nicht nur die Studenten. In allen Schichten gibt es Deutsche, die Deutschlands wirkliche Lage erkannt haben ; Goebbels schimpft sie „die Objektiven". Ob Deutschland noch selber sein Schicksal wenden kann, hängt davon ab, dass diese Menschen sich zusammenfinden und handeln. Das weiss Goebbels, und deswegen beteuert er krampfhaft, „dass diese Sorte Mensch zahlenmässig nicht ins Gewicht fällt". Sie sollen nicht wissen, wie viele sie sind.

Wir werden den Krieg sowieso gewinnen. Aber wir sehen nicht ein, warum die Vernünftigen und Anständigen in Deutschland nicht zu Worte kommen sollen. Deswegen werfen die Flieger der RAF zugleich mit ihren Bomben jetzt dieses Flugblatt, für das sechs junge Deutsche gestorben sind, und das die Gestapo natürlich sofort konfisziert hat, in Millionen von Exemplaren über Deutschland ab.

Manifest der Münchner Studenten

Erschüttert steht unser Volk vor dem Untergang der Männer von Stalingrad. 330.000 deutsche Männer hat die geniale Strategie des Weltkriegsgefreiten sinn- und verantwortungslos in Tod und Verderben gehetzt. Führer, wir danken Dir !

Es gärt im deutschen Volk. Wollen wir weiter einem Dilettanten das Schicksal unserer Armeen anvertrauen ? Wollen wir den niedrigsten Machtinstinkten einer Parteiclique den Rest der deutschen Jugend opfern ? Nimmermehr !

Der Tag der Abrechnung ist gekommen, der Abrechnung unserer deutschen Jugend mit der verabscheuungswürdigsten Tyrannei, die unser Volk je erduldet hat. Im Namen des ganzen deutschen Volkes fordern wir von dem Staat Adolf Hitlers die persönliche Freiheit, das kostbarste Gut der Deutschen zurück, um das er uns in der erbärmlichsten Weise betrogen hat.

In einem Staat rücksichtsloser Knebelung jeder freien Meinungsäußerung sind wir aufgewachsen.

not speak up'.[140] Two pamphlets inspired by the White Rose were also produced by the Red Army in June 1943, calling on German soldiers to bring an end to the war and to overthrow Hitler.[141] One declared that although the three White Rose students had died, their spirit lived on 'in hundreds of thousands, in millions of young German hearts'.[142]

The BBC German Service, founded in 1938, broadcast news, talks, music and satire in German from London. It aimed to present capitulation to the Allies as an acceptable option to German listeners.[143] In June 1943 the exiled German novelist Thomas Mann dedicated one of his regular broadcasts to the White Rose, praising their heroism and declaring 'You shall not have died in vain; you shall not be forgotten.'[144] The war would roll on for another two years, but the White Rose would indeed *not* be forgotten.

THE LEGACY OF THE WHITE ROSE TODAY

Public awareness and commemoration of historical events or personages go hand in hand: where there is awareness, there are acts of commemoration, and where groups and individuals are memorialized and remembered institutionally, public awareness grows. The memory of the White Rose was kept alive in many and varied ways from the mid-1940s onwards. One of the earliest monuments to the group was erected in 1946 in the atrium of the main university building in Munich. Further memorials were created, and streets, squares and schools were renamed. Strikingly, this kind of memorialization occurred on both sides of the Berlin Wall.[145] In September 1949 the city council in Freiburg, – at that point in the Soviet occupation zone – elected to rename one of its schools the Scholl Sibling School (Geschwister-Scholl-Schule).[146]

In 1961 a stamp bearing an image of Sophie Scholl and Hans Scholl was produced in East Germany as part of a series commemorating concentration-camp victims. In West Germany in 1964 Sophie Scholl's likeness was included on one of a series of stamps issued to mark the twentieth anniversary of the 20 July 1944 attempt on Hitler's life. In 1983 the White Rose was remembered with a commemorative stamp bearing a design of barbed wire and a white rose as part of a series marking 'Persecution and Resistance 1933–1945'. Sophie Scholl appeared again on a stamp issued in reunified Germany in 1991, as part of a series commemorating significant women in German history. The number of postage stamps dedicated to the White Rose is strangely fitting, given the lengths they themselves had to go to in order to obtain stamps to distribute their resistance pamphlets.

One of the most prominent written accounts of the White Rose, first published in 1952, is the work of one of the other Scholl siblings, Inge Scholl: *Die Weiße Rose*. It is a document of witness, consisting of a first-person retrospective account by the author, as well as copies of the resistance pamphlets, documents from the first two White Rose trials and eyewitness statements. It has been published in several editions since the 1950s and first appeared in English in 1970 as *Students against Tyranny: The Resistance of the White Rose*.[147] The first academic study of the group was published in 1968 in West Germany: Christian Petry's *Students on the Scaffold: The Defeat of the White Rose* (*Studenten aufs Schafott: Die Weiße Rose und ihr Scheitern*). Since then there have been hundreds of books about the White Rose circle in German, including historical studies and biographies of the central figures. There have also been several works in English, including not only historical studies, but novels, fictional retellings for children and teenagers, and, most recently, a graphic novel.[148]

It was arguably from the 1980s onwards that commemoration of the White Rose became more securely rooted within public and institutional memory. This was thanks in part to the first publication of selected letters and diary entries by members of the group, both in German and in English.[149] The White Rose was also immortalized in film. In 1982 two adaptations of the history appeared in West Germany: Percy Adlon's *Five Last Days*, which was broadcast on West German television, and Michael Verhoeven's feature film *The White Rose*, which was an unmitigated box office hit. The same actress, Lena Stolze, plays Sophie Scholl in both productions. Verhoeven's film was significant in exposing a bizarre legal situation: a closing title declared that the sentences against the White Rose were still considered legal by the Federal Court since the Nazi court's decisions had never been formally rescinded. There was a public outcry and in 1985 the German parliament passed a resolution negating the verdicts.

If you visit Munich today, you will find traces of the White Rose throughout the city. Plaques commemorate

Pavement memorial by the artist Robert Schmidt-Matt, erected in
1988 on the Geschwister-Scholl-Platz outside the Ludwig Maximilian
University in Munich.

the apartments where the participants lived, and a memorial to their memory can be found just minutes away from the city's major shopping district. The squares in front of the main university building where Hans and Sophie left copies of the sixth leaflet is named after them, and the square opposite commemorates Professor Kurt Huber. In front of the main building there is a pavement memorial by the artist Robert Schmidt-Matt composed of printed copies of the leaflets and photographs of the group's members etched in stone and set into the cobblestones. Inside, a bronze relief commemorates all seven members who were executed, and there is a bronze bust of Sophie Scholl. An annual organ concert and other events, as well as a permanent exhibition, the *DenkStätte Weiße Rose*, keep the memory of the White Rose alive in the university and beyond.

Travel about an hour and a half north of Munich and you will find the Walhalla memorial, an imposing neoclassical building set high above the Danube river, filled with plaques, busts and statues of 'noted Germans'. Here, among the great and the good of German history, you will find a marble bust of Sophie Scholl, dedicated to those who resisted fascism.[150] There is even a waxwork of Sophie Scholl in the Berlin branch of Madame Tussauds alongside a figure of Anne Frank. Multiple buildings including schools have been named after all six members of the core group, while 'Scholl Sibling School' is the most popular school name in Germany. One of Germany's leading literary awards, the Scholl Siblings Prize (*Geschwister-Scholl-Preis*), is awarded annually by the State Association of Bavaria for a book that 'promotes civic freedom, moral, intellectual and aesthetic courage, and fosters a responsible awareness of present-day issues'.[151] Past recipients include the philosopher Jürgen Habermas (b.1929), the East German author Christa Wolf (1929–2011) and Helmuth James Graf von Moltke, who smuggled out the sixth White Rose pamphlet, and who was awarded the prize posthumously for his book *Letters to Freya 1939–1945* (1988).

In 2003 a series broadcast on the German television channel ZDF had a competition to find the nation's favourite German: 'Our Best — The Greatest Germans'. In the final vote, Konrad Adenauer (first chancellor of West Germany, 1949–63) achieved the top spot, followed by Martin Luther and Karl Marx, and then in fourth position by Hans Scholl and Sophie Scholl. In 2005 Marc Rothemund's film *Sophie Scholl — The Final Days* was released. The film-makers were able to make use of the substantial archival material thought lost after the war, including the transcripts of the White Rose Gestapo interrogations. The film received multiple awards and was nominated for an Oscar for Best Foreign Language Film. It was certainly this treatment of the story in film that provided a renewed interest in the story, especially in the English-speaking world.

In January 1945 Theodor Haecker wrote in his diary that 'no one feels so disgustingly certain of victory, or is so unteachably sure, and immune to reason, as the fanatic, and that no one is so absolutely certain of ultimate defeat.'[152] The individuals at the heart of the White Rose had seen up close the effects of such fanaticism. They lost friends and comrades, witnessed persecution, and feared what a Nazi victory would mean, not only for Germany but for Europe and the world. Their pamphlets were designed to stir up the people, confronting them with truths that the group believed they were deliberately ignoring, through fear or, worse, through obstinacy or ambivalence. They spoke of freedom, moral duty, corruption, evil and the urgent need for action. They levelled powerful accusations at their readers. They were angry, idealistic, unwavering and uncompromising. Helmuth James Graf von Moltke said in a report on the White Rose that it represented 'a clear case of internal revolt, based on moral principles of the highest order'.[155]

The White Rose members were, in some ways, ideologically aligned with other resistance circles in Germany at the time, and even sought to forge connections with other dissidents and opponents of Nazism. In Berlin the Kreisau Circle (Kreisauer Kreis) gathered around Helmuth James Graf von Moltke and Peter Graf Yorck von Wartenberg, both members of the Prussian nobility. A group of around twenty individuals from diverse backgrounds met intermittently over the course of three years. They attended conferences at the Kreisau estate in Silesia (now Krzyżowa, Poland). Like the White Rose, they were concerned with what would happen when the war ended and developed a programme for the future governance of Germany. Their discussions presupposed German defeat in the Second World War and for this reason their activities were condemned by the regime as treasonous. Yorck's cousin, Claus von Stauffenberg, led a plot to assassinate Hitler on 20 July 1944. The plot failed and the plotters were arrested, including Yorck, who was identified as one of those involved. Both Yorck and von Moltke were tried under Roland Freisler and executed on 23 January 1945. Like the White Rose, the Kreisau Circle did not effect much material change during the Third Reich itself. Instead, it gained significance after the war, by virtue of having been an attempt to unify those with contrasting views to develop a vision of a new, democratic Germany.[154]

The Red Orchestra was an umbrella term applied by the German military intelligence organization (*Abwehr*) to a range of resistance groups. The name derived from the fact that members were accused of transmitting military secrets to the Soviets. The Berlin circle gathered around Arvid Harnack and his wife Mildred Fish-Harnack, and Harro Schulze-Boysen and his wife Libertas Schulze-Boysen. The resistance consisted of a network of around 130 individuals, again with very diverse backgrounds, whose activities included writing and distributing pamphlets and letters and passing military intelligence to the Soviets.[155] In 1942 more than a hundred of the members of the network were rounded up by the Gestapo. Over half of them were sent to concentration camps, and the others executed, including the Schulze-Boysens and the Harnacks. On Tuesday, 16 February 1943, just two days before the first arrests of the White Rose members, Mildred Fish-Harnack was executed at Plötzensee Prison in Berlin.[156] She was the only American citizen to be executed on Hitler's direct orders.

Questions are often asked about how much of an impact the White Rose had. There has been criticism of their youthful impetuosity and the risks they took.

Some have questioned how much concrete change they really achieved. Yet, as Annette Dumbach and Jud Newborn write in their history of the group, it is impossible to calculate the influence of the White Rose: 'their significance is deeper; it goes even beyond the Third Reich, beyond Germany'.[157] It is the legacy of the White Rose, their impact after their deaths and their place in the memory and history of modern Germany that make them so significant.

One of the first published accounts in English of the White Rose was William Bayles's *Seven Were Hanged*, published in London in 1945. It is an imaginative account, based on the testimony of a university student from Munich who had escaped Germany. It has a preface written by Eleanor F. Rathbone (1872–1946), Member of Parliament for the Combined English Universities, vocal anti-Nazi and active supporter of the rights of women and families. In this short preface she addresses the reader directly, posing a question that has been at the centre of post-war discussions about the Third Reich and its memory:

> if you still condemn the Germans for what they did *not* do to overthrow Hitler, ask yourself what *you* would have done, were you a German. ... Would you, like the Munich students, or the plotters against Hitler's life, or the nameless victims of the concentration camps, have risked all this?[158]

The White Rose impels us to ask questions about our own times, not as a reductive historical parallel, but as inspiration or an impetus to examine one's own circumstances. It leads us to ask what makes it possible for individuals, even those who have been indoctrinated by a pernicious political ideology, to see through it and stand up against it, even if that means death? The pamphlets of the White Rose are part of a much larger story about the power of the written word beyond the German context, and ultimately how culture can inform political action.

Sophie Scholl with her brother Hans (*left*) and Christoph Probst (*right*) at the *Ostbahnhof* station in Munich on 23 July 1942.

BIOGRAPHICAL SKETCHES

SOPHIE SCHOLL (1921–1943)

Sophie Scholl was born on 9 May 1921 to Robert
Scholl (1891–1973) and Magdalena Scholl, née Müller
(1881–1958). She was one of six siblings, the youngest of
whom died in infancy. The children were brought up in a
household shaped by liberal and Christian values. Their
father, a pacifist and anti-fascist, opposed Nazism. Never-
theless, the Scholl children, including Sophie, became
active in the Hitler Youth. Indeed, when Sophie Scholl
and her brother Werner were confirmed on Palm Sunday
1937 they were the only children wearing their Hitler
Youth uniforms.[1] However, Sophie came to reject Nazism
as she understood more about its ideology and saw how it
marginalized and persecuted the innocent. A story is told
about Sophie and one of her favourite writers, Heinrich
Heine. An important leader of the League of German
Girls visited the local group in Ulm where the Scholls
lived. At this meeting Sophie reportedly suggested
that they read and discuss poems by Heine. The leader,
obviously appalled at the idea, declared that Heine was
a Jewish writer whose works had been banned. Sophie
Scholl is said to have retorted: 'Anyone who doesn't know
Heine doesn't know German literature.'[2]

While still at school in 1937 she had attended a dance where she met the young air force soldier Fritz Hartnagel (1917–2001). They developed a close romantic friendship, writing often and seeing each other when they could. This was increasingly infrequently as the war progressed. The two were able to meet while Fritz was on leave in May 1942. This was the last time they would see each other. Their correspondence speaks of their developing relationship, which was shaped by a lively exchange of ideas and feelings, and traces their engagement with external forces and their shifting stances towards Nazism.

On 9 April 1940, while she was at home in Ulm, Sophie wrote to Hartnagel:

> Sometimes I dread the war and I'm on the brink of losing all hope. I don't even want to think about it, but soon there won't be anything but politics, and as long as politics is this confused and evil, turning away from it would be cowardly. You're probably smiling now and thinking 'she's such a girl'. But I think I'd be far happier if I weren't constantly under all this pressure – I could spend time doing other things with a much clearer conscience. But everything else comes second now. It's just that we've been brought up to be political. (Now you'll be laughing again.) I just want to be with you again and see and feel nothing but the fabric of your suit. Is this a bad letter? It's not a breath of fresh air in your musty room, in fact it's probably making it even mustier. Don't hold it against me.[3]

This letter was written on the day that German troops invaded Denmark. The following month Sophie completed her school leaving certificate and, after training as a kindergarten teacher, undertook compulsory labour service (*Arbeitsdienst*) in Krauchenwies and then another six months of war service (*Kriegshilfsdienst*) in Blumberg. She found this period difficult, to say the least. She loved literature, music, art, philosophy and religion, and found the authoritarian structures and rigidity unpalatable and was frustrated by her fellow recruits. In May 1942 she was finally able to begin studying biology and philosophy at the Ludwig Maximilian University in Munich. Here she joined her brother and was inducted into his circle of friends and mentors.

Sophie was a central figure in the White Rose circle, helping to obtain resources and participating in the logistics of the pamphlet campaign, including distributing copies at great personal risk.[4] In her interrogation by Gestapo official Robert Mohr she was asked whether she regarded what she, her brother and their friends had done as a crime against the people and against the troops fighting in the east that deserved strongest condemnation. She replied:

> I remain of the opinion that I did the best I could for my people. I therefore have no regrets about my conduct and accept the consequences that will arise from my conduct.[5]

Sophie Scholl was tried alongside Hans Scholl and Christoph Probst on Monday, 22 February 1943. When she was taken to the Palace of Justice that morning, she had left a copy of the court's indictment in her cell on which she had written one word: 'Freedom'.[6] She was executed at 5 p.m. later that day. She was 21 years old.

Hans Scholl, c.1942.

HANS SCHOLL (1918–1943)

Hans Scholl was born on 22 September 1918, just as the
First World War was approaching its end. Hans was the
first of his siblings to join the Hitler Youth in March 1933,
before membership became compulsory and against
the wishes of his father. Hans Scholl became the leader
of a squad of around 150 boys (*Fähnleinführer*),[7] and in
September 1935 was a torch-bearer at the annual Nuremberg Rally. His enthusiasm for the Hitler Youth waned,
however, and he became disillusioned by National Socialism. Inge Scholl recounted an episode that gives a sense
of how this process might have occurred. Hans Scholl
was reading a volume by his then favourite author, Stefan
Zweig (1881–1942), an Austrian Jew who left Austria following Hitler's rise to power. Hans's Hitler Youth leader
saw what he was reading, a collection of historical minia-
tures about events that changed history, and reportedly
snatched the book out of his hands. Hans Scholl was told
that the book was banned. When he asked why, he was
not given an answer.[8] The content of the text was un-
important. Only the identity of its author mattered.

Hans Scholl completed his school leaving certificate
(*Abitur*) in 1937. He then spent seven months undertaking compulsory labour service (*Arbeitsdienst*), and in
November 1937 joined a cavalry regiment for six months
of training to become a medical orderly. On 13 December 1937 he was arrested at his barracks. Two charges
were levelled at him: first, that he had been involved in
'subversive activities' as part of a youth movement, for
having been part of a banned youth group known as the
'd.j.1.11' (Deutsche Jungenschaft, 1 November); second,

that he had engaged in 'prosecutable actions' (code for homosexual activities) with another boy when he was 16.[9] He was acquitted as part of an amnesty that followed Germany's annexation of Austria on 12 March 1938.

He completed his basic military training on 1 November 1938 and began his studies in April 1939 at the university in Munich after completing an army medical corps course. In the vacation he was forced to do 'voluntary work', harvesting in East Prussia. He then enrolled for his second term in October 1939. In March 1940 he was drafted into the Wehrmacht and stationed in Kassel and then Bad Sooden. He was able to continue his studies at the university in Göttingen during this period. Germany invaded the Netherlands and Belgium on 10 May 1940. On 15 May his student company was deployed to the Western Front. On 22 June 1940 the Franco-German armistice was signed, and in September 1940 Hans Scholl returned to Germany and resumed his studies in Munich in October. It was at this point that he met Alexander Schmorell, who was also studying medicine. In January 1941 Hans passed the preliminary medical exam and, in the summer, he began an internship at a hospital in Harlaching in Munich where Alexander Schmorell was also working. In the summer of 1941 Hans was introduced to Carl Muth by Otl Aicher and worked cataloguing Muth's library. The conversations he had with Muth and, through him, with other intellectuals such as Haecker were profoundly important in developing his sense of opposition to National Socialism. His internship ended in October; after two weeks' vacation the new term began in November 1941.

Hans was the driving force behind the White Rose circle. He loved literature and philosophy, read widely, was musical and wrote poetry. He also had a good sense of humour. In a letter to his parents and sister in March 1942, for example, he wondered aloud whether they had been receiving his letters, because the post was very 'disorganized'. He then added with more than a hint of mischief that he rather pitied the Gestapo for having to decipher quantities of illegible handwriting, but that after all, it was their job and their duty.[10]

In the course of his interrogations by the Gestapo in February 1943 he set out the reasons for his actions: 'I believed I was compelled to act from an inner drive and thought that this inner obligation stood above the oath of allegiance that I had made as a soldier.'[11] Hans Scholl was executed on Monday, 22 February 1943. He was buried next to his sister, Sophie Scholl, and Christoph Probst in the cemetery at Perlacher Forst, Munich.

CHRISTOPH PROBST (1919–1943)

Hermann Christoph Ananda Probst, known affectionately as 'Christel', was born on 6 November 1919 in Murnau in southern Germany to Hermann Probst (1886–1936) and Katharina Probst, née von der Bank (1889–1963). His parents had separated four months before he was born and divorced in 1922, after which he and his older sister, Angelika (1918–1976), lived between the two parental homes. In 1923 Katharina Probst married Eugen Sasse, and they had a son, Dieter (b.1924). In 1928 Hermann Probst married Elise Jaffée (née Rosenthal). Christoph

Christoph Probst with his son Michael, c.1942.

Probst's childhood was unconventional and richly influenced by avant-garde culture. The family were friends with artists Paul Klee, Emil Nolde, Gabriele Münter and Marie Marc. Hermann Probst was an independent scholar with interests in Sanskrit, Indian philosophy, transcendentalism and expressionism.[12] It was by all accounts a time of early childhood dominated by love, affection and an emphasis on free-thinking and freedom of self-expression.

In 1932 Christoph Probst's mother and stepfather separated, and she moved with the three children to Marquartstein in south-east Bavaria. During this period Probst joined the Hitler Youth.[13] In March 1935, aged 15, he moved schools to the Neues Realgymnasium in Munich, where he was in the same class as Alexander Schmorell and the two became friends.[14] In the spring of 1936 Probst moved school again. Then, on 29 May 1936, his father committed suicide while he was staying at a private psychiatric clinic. Christoph was 16 years old. A school report from this period describes him as 'quite a character, sensible and wise beyond his years'.[15] Even after his father's death, Christoph Probst maintained a close relationship with his stepmother. As the wife of an Aryan German, Elise Probst, who was Jewish, had been largely shielded from the effects of the Nuremberg Laws. While this protection no longer existed after her husband's death, she survived the war thanks, it seems, to the unwillingness of anyone in her local community to denounce her.[16] For Christoph Probst, however, anti-Semitism and the effects of Nazi race laws were a concrete reality and close to home.

Probst finished school in 1937 and completed labour service, military service in the air force (Luftwaffe) and a stint in the ambulance service. In April 1939 he began his studies in medicine at the Ludwig Maximilian University in Munich and was part of a student company in the air force. On 19 August 1941, when he was 21 years old, Christoph Probst married Herta Dohrn (1914–2016), with whom he had three children: Michael (b.1940), Vincent (b.1941) and Katherina (b.January 1943). Alexander

Schmorell and Christoph Probst's sister Angelika were witnesses at the wedding.

In October 1941 Probst had to transfer to the newly established University of the Reich in Strasbourg. A month later his mother married again. Christoph was able to resume his studies in Munich in the summer semester of 1942. In December 1942 he was transferred to a student company in Innsbruck in Austria. He continued to travel back to Munich to assist with the resistance activities.

On 28 or 29 January 1943 Christoph wrote the draft pamphlet that would cost him his life, and on 31 January gave it to Hans Scholl, who had it in his pocket when he was arrested. Christoph Probst was unaware of the Scholls' arrest when, on Saturday, 20 February, he was apprehended at his barracks as he was collecting a leave permit to visit his wife and month-old daughter.[17] He was transported to Munich where he was held in the Gestapo prison at the Wittelsbach Palace and interrogated. He confessed to having written the draft pamphlet found on Hans Scholl and to having listened to enemy radio stations. When asked his position on National Socialism, he emphasized that he was not a political person and that 'At heart, I live entirely for my family.'[18] He claimed to have written the draft in a terrible state of depression following the defeat at Stalingrad and in the wake of his wife's illness following the birth of their third child.

During the first White Rose trial on Monday, 22 February no account was taken of Christoph Probst's position as a father of three young children. In a letter to his wife, Herta, on the day of his execution he wrote:

Never have I drawn so much strength from my love for you as I do now. It feels as though I am very close to you. I see you before me, I feel your love in me and my love in you and I am so happy, because I know that this love is indestructible. Even if you cannot understand why I am being held in this cell, then stay calm, stay calm and do not worry. I am being treated well, and I am not finding life in the cells so bad. And the children? I see them in my mind, one after another, so sweet, carefree and wonderfully innocent. What darling creatures you have borne me, my darling wife.... My love for you often rises beyond measure, I am unendingly grateful to you. I want to live for you and the children.[19]

Christoph was buried in the cemetery at Perlacher Forst on Wednesday, 24 February 1943. He was 23 years old.

ALEXANDER SCHMORELL (1917–1943)

Alexander Schmorell was born on 16 September 1917 in Orenburg, Russia, in the southern Urals, to a German father, Hugo Schmorell (1878–1964), and Russian mother, Natalya Schmorell, née Petrovna Vvedenskaya (1890–1918). Following the death of Alexander Schmorell's mother of typhus in 1918, his father married Elisabeth Hofmann (1892–1982) in 1920, a German who had also grown up in Orenburg. The turmoil in Russia following the Bolshevik Revolution and the Treaty of Brest-Litovsk finally resulted in the Schmorells' return to Germany. In the spring of 1921 they moved to Munich, bringing only what they could carry. They had lost everything and had to start again. The family consisted of Alexander, his

Alexander Schmorell at Marienau in northern Germany, 1941.

father and stepmother, his Russian nanny Feodora Lap-
schina (1884/85–1960), whom he called Njanja, and Hugo
Schmorell's half-sister, Emilia Oberländer (1868–1923),
who had multiple sclerosis.[20] In August 1921 Alexander's
half-brother, Erich Georg Schmorell, was born. In 1925
his half-sister, Natalie (known as Natascha), was born.

Alexander Schmorell, known to his friends as 'Schurik'
or 'Alex', grew up bilingually and in two cultures. He

completed his school leaving certificate (*Abitur*) in 1937, and then embarked on a period of compulsory national labour service, working on the construction of a stretch of the autobahn. He and Christoph Probst, who had become friends when they were in the same school class in 1935, both volunteered for military service in 1937 with the aim of getting it behind them as quickly as possible. Alexander joined an artillery regiment and trained as a gunner. However, after four weeks he requested that he be released from the military. The requirement that he swear an oath of loyalty to Adolf Hitler had proved impossible for him. It provoked a profound crisis of conscience and exposed the tensions he felt between his love for Russia and sense of loyalty to Germany. His request was refused, but there were no further repercussions.[21] From that point on, he reluctantly accepted and endured his military service. During this period he also suffered romantically. He was in love with Christoph Probst's sister Angelika, but she married Bernhard Knoop (1908–1994), a teacher, in February 1938. Alexander's regiment was deployed during the annexation of Austria in spring 1938, as well as in the Sudetenland. He was released from the military in March 1939 and began his studies in medicine at the university in Hamburg, where he got to know another medical student, Traute Lafrenz. In spring 1940 he was dispatched as a medical orderly to the Western Front in France. In the autumn he resumed his studies, now in Munich, where he met Hans Scholl.

Alexander Schmorell was an accomplished artist, sculptor and musician. He read widely and enthusiastically, especially Russian literature. He was idealistic, passionate and exuberant. For Schmorell, the German offensive against Russia in June 1941 represented an attack on his motherland, and he was immune to Nazi propaganda that demanded the Russians be viewed as 'subhuman'. In his last letter from prison, addressed to his father and stepmother on the day of his execution, he wrote:

> It seems it was not to be any other way, and in accordance with the will of God I am to leave my earthly life today, to enter another, one which will never end and where we will all meet again. May this reunion be your solace and your hope. Sadly, this will be harder for you than for me, because I pass on in the knowledge that I have remained faithful to my deepest convictions, and the truth. All of this allows me to face the imminent hour of my death with a clear conscience. ... Think of the millions of young people losing their lives out there on the battlefield – my fate is the same as theirs. In a few hours I will be in a better life, by my mother's side, and I will not forget you, and will ask God to grant you comfort and peace. And I'll be waiting for you! Above all, my parting message is this: Do not forget God!!!
>   Your Schurik.
> (With me goes Prof. Huber, who asked me to pass on his warmest greetings to you!).[22]

Alexander Schmorell was buried in the cemetery at Perlacher Forst, not far from the Scholl siblings and Christoph Probst. In February 2012 he was proclaimed a saint in the Russian Orthodox Church: Alexander of Munich.

KURT HUBER (1893–1943)

Kurt Ivo Theodor Huber was born on 24 October 1893 in Chur, Switzerland, the second of four children. In 1896 the family moved to Stuttgart in Germany where he would spend the greater part of his childhood and youth. He was a gifted child, especially musically, playing the piano and composing from a young age. As a child he was afflicted with both rickets and diphtheria, as a result of which he suffered from paralysis in his left foot, right hand and face.[23] He also had a stammer. In 1911 his father died of stomach cancer, and the family moved to Munich. Huber completed his school leaving certificate (*Abitur*) in 1912 and in the autumn began his studies in musicology, philosophy and psychology at the Ludwig Maximilian University in Munich. When the First World War broke out, he attempted to join up, but was declared unfit. In 1917 he was awarded a doctorate for research on the Italo-Dutch Renaissance composer Ivo de Vento (1544–1575) and achieved his post-doctoral qualification (*Habilitation*) in 1920 for work exploring the way music is perceived by listeners. It was published in 1923.

He began teaching at the university in 1921, and in 1926 was appointed as a non-stipendiary lecturer (*Privatdozent*). In 1929 he married Clara Schlickenrieder (1908–1998), and they had two children: Birgit, born in 1931, and Wolfgang ('Wolfi'), born in 1939. Huber was a dedicated and prolific scholar and polymath, with research interests ranging from experimental and applied psychology to Renaissance composition. In philosophy, Huber lectured on Kant, Hegel, Schelling, Leibniz and others.[24] Clara Huber later recalled that 'he would

Professor Kurt Huber.

work late into the night' and 'almost even while he was asleep'.[25] He cared deeply about his students,[26] and he was a popular lecturer, including with the student members of the White Rose. Despite his efforts, Huber was never appointed to a permanent university position or a professorship (*Lehrstuhl*), likely because he was deemed 'politically unreliable'.[27]

In addition to his other academic interests, Huber made an intensive study of folk song.[28] In 1925 he had been commissioned to collect traditional folk songs for the German Academy in Munich. In collaboration with the folk singer Emanuel Kiem, known as 'Chiem Pauli', (1882–1960), he collected and published Bavarian folk melodies.[29] In 1936 he represented Germany at the International Congress for Folk Music in Barcelona, and in 1937 he was appointed to a position in Berlin, as head of the newly established Folk Music Department at the National Institute for German Musicology (Staatliches Institut für deutsche Musikforschung). This appointment promised to bring professional and personal security for Huber. However, after just a year he was dismissed for 'ideological reasons'.[30] He had failed to show sufficient commitment to the National Socialist cause.

In June 1942 Huber met Hans Scholl at a reading evening[31] and became actively involved in the pamphlet campaign in December 1942.[32] Following the execution of the Scholls and Christoph Probst, Huber was arrested on 27 February and taken first to the Gestapo prison at the Wittelsbach Palace and then to Neudeck prison in Munich. His interrogations lasted until 10 March.[33] During this time he continued to work on his academic projects, including a biography of the philosopher Gottfried Wilhelm Leibniz (1646–1716). Although he was executed before he could finish it, the work was published posthumously. While he worked away in his cell, the university stripped him of his doctorate, title and pension.

The day before his trial, Kurt Huber wrote to his wife Clara: 'If I should suffer death in the fight for freedom, rejoice and be glad at one who has found his way home in the ultimate freedom of the spirit. Giving up my life will have made me completely free.'[34] Huber was tried on 19 April 1943 alongside Alexander Schmorell, Willi Graf and eleven other defendants. During sentencing, Huber was referred to as 'a blemish against German scholarship'.[35] The presiding judge, Roland Freisler, declared: 'The days when every man can be allowed to profess his own political "beliefs" are past. For us there is but one standard: the National Socialist one. Against this we measure each man!'[36] In his defence speech, Huber gave answer: 'My actions and desires will be justified by the iron course of history, of that I am absolutely certain.'[37] On 13 July 1943 Huber received the news of his execution and wrote to Clara Huber and the children:

> In the middle of my work for you today, I received the news that I have so long been waiting for. Dearest, rejoice with me! I may do it for my fatherland, for a just and more beautiful fatherland that will certainly arise out of this war. Dearest Clara! Your life was a thorny path, but today you are already a saint. Forgive me all the ways in which I have failed you! I love you from the depths of my heart and will be with you and our dear children every day, until you follow after me to the place where no one ever parts again. I place into your devoted and loving hands the fate and education of our dear children. I know that they will think of their father and

will give as much joy as they can to their dear mummy. Dear Clara! Death parts us just at the moment when we are closest. ... Think of the wonderful hours, of our being together with the children, and forget all suffering! We will remain one heart and one soul. ... Be proud that you are playing your part in the fight for a new Germany. You are heroes just like the women and children who lost their fathers at the Front. ... Dearest Birgit, the beginning of your life has been dark and serious, but the future is bright. Yours and mummy's letters have been an endless source of comfort to me. I know you will continue to be your mother's strength and stay. Your father will not forget you; he is praying for you all. God has given you rich gifts. Use them. Take delight in music and poetry and remain the good little angel that you have been to us. Dearest, brave little Wolfi! A whole beautiful life lies open before you. You will be a good little boy and an accomplished man, mother's protector and pride. And if life is ever difficult, think of your daddy who never stops caring for his little boy. Dear ones! Do not weep for me — I am happy and at peace![38]

An appeal for clemency was rejected, and Huber was executed at Stadelheim Prison on 13 July 1943. In 1953 the university restored his doctorate, and today one of the two squares outside the main university building bears his name. Of the poems Kurt Huber wrote while he was incarcerated, this was perhaps his last:

And when I ask myself: What have I left behind?
Ideas. Only sketches, piles of paper.
Hardly a clean copy among them. Death
Is the clean copy of my life, and that was not in vain.[39]

Willi Graf in Wehrmacht uniform.

WILLI GRAF (1918–1943)

Wilhelm Graf was born on 2 January 1918 to Gerhard Graf (1885–1951) and Anna Graf, née Gölden (1885–1954), and grew up in Saarbrücken near the French border. The family were devout Catholics and Willi was a pious child and an enthusiastic altar server. He had two older sisters, Anneliese (1921–2009) and Mathilde (1915–2001).[40] In 1929 he joined the youth federation 'New Germany' (Neudeutschland), a Catholic student group that was banned by the Nazis in 1933. In 1934 he joined the Grey Order (Der Graue Orden), another Catholic youth association that was in turn outlawed. He refused to join the Hitler Youth.

Willi Graf completed his secondary school leaving certificate (*Abitur*) in 1937 and spent six months undertaking national labour service. He then began his studies in medicine at the University of Bonn in November 1937. On 22 January 1938 he was arrested by the Gestapo[41] and spent three weeks in prison, charged with having undertaken 'subversive activities' as part of a youth movement.[42] The trial, at which he and seventeen other members of the Grey Order were due to be tried, was cancelled as part of the same amnesty that had saved Hans Scholl from prosecution. When the war broke out the university in Bonn closed and he transferred to Munich. In January 1940 he was drafted into the Wehrmacht as a medical orderly and from September 1940 to March 1941 served in France and Belgium. He was then deployed to the Eastern Front, where he was part of the campaign in Serbia and Poland, and then in Russia.[43]

Willi Graf was a voracious reader, enjoying Russian, German and French literature, and philosophy. He loved music, sang in the Munich Bach choir, and played the viola. He also fenced, attended Mass regularly and was interested in church liturgy. By all accounts he was a quiet, thoughtful and reflective young man. Following his period of service at the front, he was finally able to resume his studies in Munich in April 1942. He was part of the Second Student Company and was introduced to Hans Scholl's circle in June by Christoph Probst.[44] In his diary Graf commented succinctly: 'Conversation with Hans Scholl. Hopefully I'll see him more often.'[45] In the summer and autumn of 1942 he was deployed along with Hans Scholl, Alexander Schmorell and another friend, Hubert Furtwängler, to the Russian front. This was a profoundly important time for him; unlike his previous posting to Russia, this time he saw the country and its people through the eyes of his good friend Alexander Schmorell.

In November 1942 they arrived back in Munich and the pamphlet campaign resumed. Graf now took an active role, which principally involved travelling and finding like-minded students who would contribute to the cause. On 20 January 1943 Willi Graf travelled to Cologne, Bonn, Saarbrücken, Freiburg and Ulm to connect with others who might assist in the resistance.[46] He met with limited success.[47] He also distributed copies of the fifth pamphlet. On 3, 8 and 15 February, along with Hans Scholl and Alexander Schmorell, he painted anti-Nazi slogans on buildings in the centre of Munich.

He and his sister Anneliese, who was also a student in Munich, were arrested in the flat they shared late on the evening of 18 February.[48] He was interrogated until 23 March.[49] On 29 April his parents were permitted to visit their son in prison for the one and only time. Willi Graf was tried alongside Alexander Schmorell and Kurt Huber on 19 April 1943 and like them was sentenced to death. He was kept in solitary confinement for six months in Stadelheim prison as the Gestapo attempted, unsuccessfully, to extract further information from him.[50] In his last letter, dictated to the Catholic prison chaplain, he spoke of his deep religious faith: 'For us, death is not the end, but the beginning of our true life, and I shall die trusting in God's will and provision.'[51] He reminded his sister of the aria 'I know that my redeemer liveth' from Handel's *Messiah* that they had heard at a concert in December: 'This faith alone strengthens and sustains me. Do not forget me and pray that God will judge me mercifully.'[52] He also stressed that others should now take up the mantle of the White Rose: 'They should carry on what we have begun.'[53]

Graf was executed on the afternoon of 12 October 1943. His family was not informed of his death. One of the prison employees reportedly contacted a relative of the family in Munich secretly, who then telephoned his parents in Saarbrücken to tell them the news.[54] Willi Graf was buried in the Perlacher Forst cemetery in Munich directly opposite Stadelheim prison. After the war his body was moved to the Saint Johann cemetery in Saarbrücken. A cause is open in the Roman Catholic Church for his beatification.

Hans Leipelt.

HANS LEIPELT (1921–1945)

Hans Konrad Leipelt was born on 18 July 1921 in Vienna to Katharina Leipelt, née Baron (1892–1943) and Konrad Leipelt (1886–1942). In 1938 he completed his school leaving certificate (*Abitur*) and began national labour service. From April to October 1938 he was deployed to the construction of the Siegfried Line, a German defensive line along the Western Front which ran from the Netherlands to Switzerland. He was then part of an infantry regiment deployed to Poland and France, and in June 1940 was decorated with the Iron Cross Second Class and 'Panzer Badge in Bronze'. Two months later, however, he was dismissed from the Wehrmacht with a dishonourable discharge. As the son of a Jewish mother and non-Jewish father, he was classed as a 'Mischling' of the first degree (*Mischling ersten Grades*) by the state according to the Act for the Protection of German Blood and German Honour passed in 1935. In autumn 1940 he began his studies in chemistry at the University of Hamburg. However, after a year and a half he left due to growing anti-Semitism. He transferred to the university in Munich, where the chemistry professor Heinrich Wieland (1877–1957) was actively resisting the university's regulations and taking in Jewish students to work in his laboratory. Wieland was a distinguished scientist, having won the Nobel Prize for Chemistry in 1927. It was here that Hans Leipelt met Marie-Luise Jahn (1918–2010).

In September 1942 Leipelt's father died. The protection afforded to his mother by virtue of having an Aryan spouse was gone. The threat of deportation was a constant source of anxiety. Indeed, Leipelt's grandmother,

Hermine Baron (1866–1943), was deported in July 1942 to the Theresienstadt ghetto, where she was murdered in January 1943. In February 1943 Hans Leipelt received in the post a copy of the sixth White Rose pamphlet. He showed it to Marie-Luise Jahn, and they decided to make copies of it. In the spring vacation they took copies to Hamburg and distributed them, assisted by others, including Leipelt's sister, Maria Leipelt (1925–2008). They also collected money for Kurt Huber's widow Clara, who had been left destitute after her husband's execution. It was while engaged in these activities that Leipelt and Jahn were denounced. Leipelt was arrested on 8 October; Jahn on the 18th. Further arrests followed. Both Leipelt's sister and mother were taken into custody. Shortly after her arrest, his mother died in custody. It is possible that she took her own life, but the precise circumstances remain unclear. It is extremely likely that, had she lived, she would have been deported.

On 13 October 1944 Leipelt, Jahn and five others were tried by the People's Court at Donauwörth in southern Germany. Jahn received a twelve-year prison sentence, thanks principally to the efforts of Leipelt, who did all he could to claim responsibility for what they had done. Leipelt was sentenced to death. He spent another three months in prison. An account by his cellmate, Heinrich Hamm, records: 'He was always full of hope and never lost courage.'[55] On the day of his execution Leipelt wrote to his sister, Maria:

I beg you, and in these last hours I will pray that you will keep this trust in God your whole life. Don't be sad on my account, if you can, and at least don't worry. ...

And now finally I ask you to forgive me for being so often unkind to you, for my egotism, and above all my tremendous lack of self-control, which has brought you into all this as well. Farewell, my dear one. Again, I commend you to God's hands. I know that we will see each other again. Your loving brother, Hans.[56]

Leipelt was executed by guillotine at Munich Stadelheim prison on 29 January 1945. He is buried in the cemetery at Perlacher Forst in Munich. Marie-Luise Jahn, who was freed by the Allies in 1945 and who died in 2010, is also buried there.

THE PAMPHLETS
OF THE WHITE ROSE

A NOTE ON THE TRANSLATIONS

The English translations of the White Rose pamphlets presented here were produced by undergraduate students at the University of Oxford as part of the White Rose Project, a research and engagement initiative bringing the story of the White Rose to English-speaking audiences.[1] While there have been many translations of the pamphlets in English, the students of the White Rose Project set out to produce a new version with two aims: first, that it should be the result of collaborative work; and second, that it should be undertaken by undergraduates around the same age as the original student authors, engaged in courses at university, working together on texts, ideas and issues. The Oxford student translators were struck by how resonant the White Rose's pamphlets are today, how vividly and forcefully they speak of freedom, injustice, oppression and personal responsibility in ways that are all too necessary in our own times. They hoped to capture something of the urgency, dynamism and force of the originals. In the German pamphlets, words and phrases are emphasized by spacing out the letters. In German this is called *Sperrschrift*. This is indicated in the English translations with small capital letters.

1

Flugblätter der Weissen Rose.

I

Nichts ist eines Kulturvolkes unwürdiger, als sich ohne Widerstand von einer verantwortungslosen und dunklen Trieben ergebenen Herrscherclique "regieren" zu lassen. Ist es nicht so, dass sich jeder ehrliche Deutsche heute seiner Regierung schämt, und wer von uns ahnt das Ausmass der Schmach, die über uns und unsere Kinder kommen wird, wenn einst der Schleier von unseren Augen gefallen ist und die grauenvollsten und jegliches Mass unendlich überschreitenden Verbrechen ans Tageslicht treten? Wenn das deutsche Volk schon so in seinem tiefsten Wesen korrumpiert und zerfallen ist, dass es ohne eine Hand zu regen, im leichtsinnigen Vertrauen auf eine fragwürdige Gesetzmässigkeit der Geschichte, das Höchste, das ein Mensch besitzt, und das ihn über jede andere Kreatur erhöht, nämlich den freien Willen, preisgibt, die Freiheit des Menschen preisgibt, selbst mit einzugreifen in das Rad der Geschichte und es seiner vernünftigen Entscheidung unterzuordnen, wenn die Deutschen so jeder Individualität bar, schon so sehr zur geistlosen und feigen Masse geworden sind, dann, ja dann verdienen sie den Untergang.

Goethe spricht von den Deutschen als einem tragischen Volke, gleich dem der Juden und Griechen, aber heute hat es eher den Anschein, als sei es eine seichte, willenlose Herde von Mitläufern, denen das Mark aus dem Innersten gesogen und nun ihres Kernes beraubt, bereit sind sich in den Untergang hetzen zu lassen. Es scheint so - aber es ist nicht so; vielmehr hat man in langsamer, trügerischer, systematischer Vergewaltigung jeden einzelnen in ein geistiges Gefängnis gesteckt, und erst, als er darin gefesselt lag, wurde er sich des Verhängnisses bewusst. Wenige nur erkannten das drohende Verderben, und der Lohn für ihr heroisches Mahnen war der Tod. Ueber das Schicksal dieser Menschen wird noch zu reden sein.

Wenn jeder wartet, bis der Andere anfängt, werden die Boten der rächenden Nemesis unaufhaltsam näher und näher rücken, dann wird auch das letze Opfer sinnlos in den Rachen des unersättlichen Dämons geworfen sein. Daher muss jeder Einzelne seiner Verantwortung als Mitglied der christlichen und abendländischen Kultur bewusst in dieser letzten Stunde sich wehren so viel er kann, arbeiten wider die Geisel der Menschheit, wider den Faschismus und jedes ihm ähnliche System des absoluten Staates. Leistet passiven Widerstand - W i d e r s t a n d - wo immer Ihr auch seid, verhindert das Weiterlaufen dieser atheistischen Kriegsmaschine, ehe es zu spät ist, ehe die letzten Städte ein Trümmerhaufen sind, gleich Köln, und ehe die letzte Jugend des Volkes irgendwo für die Hybris eines Untermenschen verblutet ist. Vergesst nicht, dass ein jedes Volk diejenige Regierung verdient, die es erträgt!

Aus Friedrich Schiller, "Die Gesetzgebung des Lykurgus und Solon".

"....Gegen seinen eigenen Zweck gehalten, ist die Gestzgebung des Lykurgus ein Meisterstück der Staats- und Menschenkunde. Er wollte einen mächtigen, in sich selbst gegründeten, unzerstörbaren Staat; politische Stärke und Dauerhaftigkeit waren das Ziel, wonach er strebte, und dieses Ziel hat er so weit erreicht, als unter seinen Umständen möglich war. Aber hält man den Zweck, welchen Lykurgus sich vorsetzte, gegen den Zweck der Menschheit, so muss eine tiefe Missbilligung an die Stelle der Bewunderung treten, die uns der erste, flüchtige Blick abgewonne hat. Alles darf dem Besten des Staates zum Opfer gebracht werden, nur dasjenige nicht, dem der Staat selbst nur als ein Mittel dient. Der Staat selbst ist niemals Zweck, er ist nur wichtig als eine bedingung, unter welcher der Zweck der Menschheit erfüllt werden kann, und dieser Zweck der Mensch-

PAMPHLETS OF THE WHITE ROSE

I

Complicity with the 'governance' of an irresponsible clique of rulers driven by their darkest urges, and complicity without resistance — nothing is more unworthy of a civilized people. Is it not so that in the present day every honourable German is ashamed of their government? And who among us can foresee the extent of the infamy that will be on us, and on our children, when the veil is one day lifted from our eyes and the most horrific crimes, crimes beyond all measure, come to light? If, in their innermost being, the German people have been corrupted and degraded enough to betray the greatest quality humanity possesses, that quality which elevates them above all other creatures – free will – without so much as lifting a finger, foolishly trusting the dubious notion that history follows its natural course; if this people can betray the freedom of humankind to intervene in the course of history and to subordinate it to its rational judgement; if the Germans, so utterly devoid of any kind of individuality, have already become such a weak and mindless horde – then, yes, they truly deserve their own demise.

The first page of the first resistance pamphlet of the White Rose, June 1942.

Goethe speaks of the Germans as a tragic people, much like the Jews or the Greeks, but these days they seem more like a shallow, spineless herd of mindless followers whose substance has been sucked out of them from within and who, robbed of their very core, allow themselves to be baited into their own demise. This seems like the truth, but it isn't; a slow, deceitful, systematic violation has locked every single one of us into a mental cage, and it is only once shackled that we become conscious of our fate. Very few recognized the impending calamity, and the reward for their heroic warnings was death. Much remains to be said about the fate of these people.

If every one of us waits for someone else to start, then the heralds of avenging Nemesis will draw ever closer until the last sacrificial victim is vainly thrown into the jaws of a demon that will never be sated. Every individual must therefore, at this, the eleventh hour, fight back as much as lies in their power with an awareness of their responsibility as a member of Christian and Western culture, must work against the scourges of humanity, against fascism and all the systems of dictatorship that resemble it. Wherever you may be, mount passive resistance — RESISTANCE — obstruct the progress of this atheistic war machine before it's too late, before, like Cologne, the last cities are left in ruins, before the last remaining youths of this nation bleed to death in some unknown place for the sake of the hubris of a subhuman. Remember that every people deserves the government it is prepared to tolerate.

From Friedrich Schiller's 'The Legislation of Lycurgus and Solon':

'Seen in the light of its chosen ends, Lycurgus' legislation is a masterpiece of political and human science. He wanted a state that was powerful, founded upon itself and indestructible; the aims he set himself were political strength and longevity, and he achieved these aims as far as was possible under the circumstances he was facing. But if one confronts the aims of Lycurgus with the aims of mankind, the admiration that a first fleeting glance sparked in us must give way to deep disapproval. One may sacrifice everything for the best of the state, with one exception: that to which the state is only a means. The state in and of itself is never the object; it is merely the necessary condition under which the purpose of mankind may be fulfilled – and this purpose is none other than the development of a person's abilities to their full extent, that is to say progress. If a state's constitution hinders the development of all the inward powers of mankind, if it hinders the progress of the *Geist*, then it is harmful and reprehensible, however well thought out and perfect a work of its kind it may be. And so its longevity comes to earn it more censure than glory; it becomes a prolonged curse; the longer it lasts, the more harmful it becomes.

... Political merit was achieved, and the ability to obtain it taught, at the extent of every moral sentiment. There was no marital love in Sparta, no mother's love, no child's love, no friendship; there were nothing but citizens, nothing but citizens' virtue.

... A state law made it a duty for Spartans to treat their slaves inhumanly; and in these wretched victims of butchery, humanity was violated and abused. The Spartan Code of Law itself preached the dangerous principle that people were to be regarded as means and not ends, thereby constitutionally obliterating the foundations of natural law and morality.

... There is no finer scene than that played out in his camp at the gates of Rome by the savage warrior Gaius Marcius who sacrificed revenge and victory because he could not bear to see his mother's tears!

... The state [of Lycurgus] could only subsist under one condition: the spirit of the nation would have to stand still; and to ensure its continued existence would therefore mean to neglect the highest and the sole aim of a state.'

From Goethe's *Epimenides Awakes*, act II, scene 4:

SPIRITS
What burst forth bold from the abyss
Could with a brazen mastery
Claim victory of half the globe –
Yet now back to the void it must.
A monstrous fear already looms,
And all resistance will be vain!
The ones who still cling on to it
Will perish with its name.

HOPE
And now I'll meet my brave of heart,
Who gather in the midst of night,
To share a silence, keep awake.
They stutter, stammer, on and on

That fair enchanting word: Freedom,
Till on our temple's steps anew
So youthful and so unfamiliar
We call its name, a joyful clamour:

    (*With conviction, loud*)
Freedom!

      (*More moderately*)
        Freedom!

      (*Echoing from all sides*)
            Freedom!

We urge you to transcribe this pamphlet, make as many
copies as you can, and distribute them!

2

Flugblätter der Weissen Rose

II

Man kann sich mit dem Nationalsozialismus geistig nicht auseinandersetzen, weil er ungeistig ist. Es ist falsch, wenn man von einer nationalsozialistischen Weltanschauung spricht, denn, wenn es diese gäbe, müsste man versuchen, sie mit geistigen Mitteln zu beweisen oder zu bekämpfen - die Wirklichkeit aber bietet uns ein völlig anderes Bild: schon in ihrem ersten Keim war diese Bewegung auf den Betrug des Mitmenschen angewiesen, schon damals war sie im Innersten verfault und konnte sich nur durch die stete Lüge retten. Schreibt doch Hitler selbst in einer frühen Auflage "seines" Buches (ein Buch, das in dem übelsten Deutsch geschrieben worden ist, das ich je gelesen habe; dennoch ist es von dem Volke der Dichter und Denker zur Bibel erhoben worden): "Man glaubt nicht, wie man ein Volk betrügen muss, um es zu regieren." Wenn sich nun am Anfang dieses Krebsgeschwür des Deutschen Volkes noch nicht allzusehr bemerkbar gemacht hatte, so nur deshalb, weil noch gute Kräfte genug am Werk waren, es zurückzuhalten. Wie es aber grösser und grösser wurde und schliesslich mittels einer letzten gemeinen Korruption zur Macht kam, das Geschwür gleichsam aufbrach und den ganzen Körper besudelte, versteckte sich die Mehrzahl der früheren Gegner, flüchtete die deutsche Intelligenz in ein Kellerloch, um dort als Nachtschattengewächs, dem Licht und der Sonne verborgen, allmählich zu ersticken. Jetzt stehen wir vor dem Ende. Jetzt kommt es darauf an, sich gegenseitig wiederzufinden, aufzuklären von Mensch zu Mensch, immer daran zu denken und sich keine Ruhe zu geben, bis auch der letzte von der äussersten Notwendigkeit seines Kämpfens wider dieses System überzeugt ist. Wenn so eine Welle des Aufruhrs durch das Land geht, wenn "es in der Luft liegt", wenn viele mitmachen, dann kann in einer letzten, gewaltigen Anstrengung dieses System abgeschüttelt werden. Ein Ende mit Schrecken ist immer noch besser, als ein Schrecken ohne Ende.

Es ist uns nicht gegeben, ein endgültiges Urteil über den Sinn unserer Geschichte zu fällen. Aber wenn diese Katastrophe uns zum Heile dienen soll, so doch nur dadurch: Durch das Leid gereinigt zu werden, aus der tiefsten Nacht heraus das Licht zu ersehnen, sich aufzuraffen und endlich mitzuhelfen, das Joch abzuschütteln, das die Welt bedrückt.

Nicht über die Judenfrage wollen wir in diesem Blatte schreiben, keine Verteidigungsrede verfassen - nein nur als Beispiel wollen wir die Tatsache kurz anführen, die Tatsache, dass seit der Eroberung Polens dreihunderttausend Juden in diesem Land auf bestialischste Art ermordet worden sind. Hier sehen wir das fürchterlichste Verbrechen an der Würde des Menschen, ein Verbrechen, dem sich kein ähnliches in der ganzen Menschengeschichte an die Seite stellen kann. Auch die Juden sind doch Menschen - man mag sich zur Judenfrage stellen wie man will - und an Menschen wurde solches verübt. Vielleicht sagt jemand, die Juden hätten ein solches Schicksal verdient; diese Behauptung wäre eine ungeheure Anmassung; aber angenommen, es sagte jemand dies , wie stellt er sich dann zu der Tatsache, dass die gesamte polnische adelige Jugend vernichtet worden ist (Gebe Gott ,dass sie es noch nicht ist!)? Auf welche Art, fragen sie, ist solches geschehen? Alle männlichen Sprösslinge aus adeligen Geschlechtern zwischen 15 und 20 Jahren wurden in Konzentrationslager nach Deutschland zu Zwangsarbeit ,alle Mädchen gleichen Alters nach Norwegen in die Bordelle der SS verschleppt !Wozu wir dies Ihnen alles erzählen, da sie es schon selber wissen, wenn nicht diese, so andere gleich schwere Verbrechen des fürchterlichen Untermenschentums? Weil hier eine Frage berührt wird, die uns alle zutiefst angeht und allen zu denken geben m u s s : Warum verhält sich das deutsche

PAMPHLETS OF THE WHITE ROSE
II

National Socialism cannot be confronted intellectually because it is not intellectual. It is wrong to speak of a National Socialist world-view, because if such a thing existed it would need to be proved or challenged by intellectual means — yet in reality we are presented with a completely different picture: even in its earliest embryonic form this movement was dependent on deceiving the German people; even then, it was rotten to the very core and could only save itself through ceaseless deception. Even Hitler himself writes in an early edition of 'his' book (a book which, despite having been written in the most appalling German that I have ever read, has been elevated to biblical status by this nation of poets and philosophers): 'You would not believe the extent to which you must deceive a people in order to govern it.' If at first this cancerous tumour on the German people had not yet made itself all too conspicuous, this was only because there were still forces for good working effectively enough to hold it back. Yet as it became bigger and bigger and finally came to power with one

The first page of the second resistance pamphlet of the White Rose, summer 1942.

last base act of corruption, the tumour, so to speak, ruptured, contaminating the whole body. The majority of its earlier opponents then went into hiding and the German intelligentsia sought refuge in a coal cellar only to gradually suffocate there, like nightshade hidden away from daylight and the sun. Now, we are approaching the end. Now, everything depends on finding one another again, on one person enlightening the next, always reflecting and never resting until every last person is convinced of the dire necessity of fighting against this system. If such a wave of uproar travels through the country, if there is 'something in the air', if many people get involved, then this system can be shaken off with one final tremendous effort. An end with terror is still better than terror without end.

It is not our place to give a final judgement on the meaning of our history. But if this catastrophe is to heal us, it will be solely by means of being purified by suffering, of yearning for the light in the very deepest darkness, by stirring ourselves, and finally by playing our part in casting off the yoke which weighs down the world.

We do not want to write about the Jewish question in this pamphlet, nor to compose a plea of defence – no, we want only to briefly point out by way of example the fact that, since the conquest of Poland, *three hundred thousand* Jews have been murdered in that country in the most bestial manner. Here, we see the most horrific crime against human dignity, a crime unparalleled in all of human history. For Jews are human beings too

– whichever stance one might take on the Jewish question – and it is against human beings that this has been committed. Some might say that the Jews deserved such a fate; this would be a claim of colossal arrogance – but, assuming that someone did say this, what stance would they then take towards the fact that the entire youth of Poland's aristocracy has been annihilated (God grant that this is not yet the case!)? How, you ask, has such a thing occurred? All the male offspring of aristocratic families between the ages of 15 and 20 were carted off to Germany for forced labour in the concentration camps, and all the girls of the same age to Norway into the brothels of the SS! Why are we telling you all this, given that you already know about it, or if not about this, then about other, equally serious crimes of this appalling subhumanity? Because it touches on an issue that deeply concerns us all and MUST give us pause for thought. Why do the German people behave so apathetically in the face of all these most atrocious, most inhumane crimes? Barely anyone gives it a thought. The fact is accepted as such and filed away. And again, the German people return to their dull, stupid sleep and give these fascist criminals the courage and the opportunity to go on rampaging — and that is precisely what they do. Should this be taken as a sign that the Germans' most primitive, human emotions have been rendered so brutal that no voice within them cries out piercingly in the face of such deeds, that they have sunk into a deadly sleep, from which there is no awakening, not ever? This is how it seems, and how it certainly will be, if Germany does not start up from this apathy, if she does not protest against this clique of criminals wherever she can, if she does not feel a collective suffering with these hundreds of thousands of victims. And she must not only feel collective suffering, no, much more: COLLECTIVE GUILT. Since, through her apathetic behaviour, she gives these dark leaders the opportunity to act this way in the first place, she suffers under this 'government', which has burdened itself with such endless guilt; yet it is her own fault that it was able to emerge in the first place! Everyone wants to exonerate themselves from such a collective guilt, everyone does so and returns to sleeping soundly with the calmest, clearest conscience. But no one can exonerate themselves, everyone is GUILTY, GUILTY, GUILTY! Yet it is not too late to rid the world of this most heinous monstrosity of a government, so we do not further yoke ourselves to guilt. Now, since our eyes have been fully opened over the last few years, since we know with whom we're dealing, it is high time to exterminate this brownshirt horde. Until the outbreak of the war, the vast majority of the German people were blinded, the National Socialists did not show their true face, but now, since they have been seen for what they are, the highest and only duty, the most sacred duty even of every German must be to destroy these beasts!

'If a regime is unobtrusive, its people are happy. If a regime is oppressive, the people are broken. Misery, alas, is what happiness is built upon. Happiness, alas, only veils misery. Where does all this lead? The end is nowhere in sight. Order lapses into disorder, good lapses into evil. The people fall into disarray. Has this not long been the case, day in, day out? Therefore, the wise man is angular, but does not scrape; he has edges, but does not hurt anyone; he stands strong, but without being harsh. He is bright, but he does not wish to gleam.'

Laozi

He who sets out to rule over the empire and to shape it as he pleases; I do not see him achieving his aim; that is all.

The empire is a living organism; in truth, it cannot be constructed! He who seeks to construct it, corrupts it, he who seeks to grasp it, loses it.

Therefore: 'Some beings go on ahead, others follow them, some have warm breath, others cold, some are strong, others weak, some reach fulfilment, others are overcome.'

The wise man therefore refrains from exaggeration, from extremes, and from excess.

Laozi

Please copy this document and distribute it as widely as possible.

3

Flugblätter der Weissen Rose

III

"Salus publica suprema lex."

Alle idealen Staatsformen sind Utopien. Ein Staat kann nicht rein theoretisch konstruiert werden, sondern er muss ebenso wachsen, reifen, wie der einzelne Mensch. Aber es ist nicht zu vergessen, dass am Anfang einer jeden Kultur die Vorform des Staates vorhanden war. Die Familie ist so alt, wie die Menschen selbst und aus diesem anfänglichen Zusammensein hat sich der vernunftbegabte Mensch einen Staat geschaffen, dessen Grund die Gerechtigkeit und dessen höchstes Gesetz das Wohl Aller sein soll. Der Staat soll eine Analogie der göttlichen Ordnung darstellen, und die höchste aller Utopien, die civitas Dei ist das Vorbild, dem er sich letzten Endes nähern soll. Wir wollen hier nicht urteilen über die verschiedenen möglichen Staatsformen, die Demokratie, die konstitutionelle Monarchie, das Königtum usw. Nur eines will eindeutig und klar herausgehoben werden: jeder einzelne Mensch hat einen Anspruch auf einen brauchbaren und gerechten Staat, der die Freiheit des Einzelnen als auch das Wohl der Gesamtheit, sichert. Denn der Mensch soll nach Gottes Willen frei und unabhängig im Zusammenleben und Zusammenwirken der staatlichen Gemeinschaft sein natürliches Ziel, sein irdisches Glück in Selbstänigkeit und Selbsttätigkeit zu erreichen suchen.

Unser heutiger "Staat" aber ist die Diktatur des Bösen. "Das wissen wir schon lange," höre ich Dich einwenden, "und wir haben es nicht nötig, dass uns dies hier noch einmal vorgehalten wird." Aber, frage ich Dich, wenn ihr das wisst, warum regt ihr euch nicht, warum duldet ihr, dass diese Gewalthaber Schritt für Schritt offen und im Verborgenen eine Domäne eures Rechtes nach der anderen rauben, bis eines Tages nichts, aber auch gar nichts übrigbleiben wird, als ein mechanisiertes Staatsgetriebe, kommandiert von Verbrechern und Säufern? Ist euer Geist schon so sehr der Vergewaltigung unterlegen, dass ihr vergesst, dass es nicht nur euer Recht, sondern eure s i t t l i c h e P f l i c h t ist, dieses System zu beseitigen? Wenn aber ein Mensch nicht mehr die Kraft aufbringt, sein Recht zu fordern, dann muss er mit absoluter Notwendigkeit untergehen. Wir würden es verdienen, in alle Welt verstreut zu werden, wie der Staub vor dem Winde, wenn wir uns in dieser zwölften Stunde nicht aufrafften und endlich den Mut aufbrächten, der uns seither gefehlt hat. Verbergt nicht eure Feigheit unter dem Mantel der Klugheit! Denn mit jedem Tag, da ihr noch zögert, da ihr dieser Ausgeburt der Hölle nicht widersteht, wächst eure Schuld gleich einer parabolischen Kurve höher und immer höher.

Viele, vielleicht die meisten Leser dieser Blätter sind sich darüber nicht klar, wie sie einen Widerstand ausüben sollen. Sie sehen keine Möglichkeiten. Wir wollen versuchen Ihnen zu zeigen, dass ein jeder in der Lage ist, etwas beizutragen zum Sturz dieses Systems. Nicht durch individualistische Gegnerschaft, in der Art verbitterter Einsiedler, wird es möglich werden, den Boden für einen Sturz dieser "Regierung" reif zu machen oder gar den Umsturz möglichst bald herbeizuführen, sondern nur durch die Zusammenarbeit vieler überzeugter, tatkräftiger Menschen, Menschen, die sich einig sind, mit welchen Mitteln sie ihr Ziel erreichen können. Wir haben keine reiche Auswahl an solchen Mitteln, nur ein einziges steht uns zur Verfügung - der p a s s i v e W i d e r s t a n d .

PAMPHLETS OF THE WHITE ROSE
III

'Salus publica suprema lex.'

All ideal forms of state are utopias. A state cannot be constructed in purely theoretical terms, but must grow and mature in the same way as every individual person. But we must not forget that an early form of the state was present at the beginning of every culture. The family is as old as humanity itself and from this original unit people, endowed with reason, created a state whose foundation was to be justice and whose supreme law was to be the common good. The state should be analogous to the divine order, and the greatest of all utopias, the Civitas Dei, is the ideal that it should ultimately resemble. We do not want to pass judgement here on the various possible forms of state: democracy, constitutional or absolute monarchy, etc. Only one thing must be made unambiguously clear: every single person is entitled to a viable and just government that ensures the freedom of the individual as well as the welfare of society as a whole. For each person should, in accordance with God's will, freely and independently seek to achieve their natural goal, that is their earthly happiness through self-reliance

The first page of the third resistance pamphlet of the White Rose, summer 1942.

and initiative, while coexisting and cooperating within the state as a community.

But our current 'state' is the dictatorship of evil. 'We know that already,' I hear you object, 'and we don't need you to reproach us for it yet again.' But, I ask you, if you know that, then why don't you act? Why do you tolerate these rulers gradually robbing you, in public and in private, of one right after another, until one day nothing, absolutely nothing, remains but the machinery of the state, under the command of criminals and drunkards? Has this violation defeated your spirit to such an extent that you have forgotten that it is not only your right but also your MORAL DUTY to do away with this system? But if a person can no longer summon the strength to demand their rights, they will certainly perish. We deserve to be scattered across the world like dust before the wind if we do not prepare ourselves for action now, at the eleventh hour, and finally muster the courage which we have thus far lacked. Do not conceal your cowardice under the cloak of expediency! For with every day that you continue to hesitate, that you do not resist this spawn of hell, your guilt grows exponentially greater.

Many, perhaps even the majority, of those reading these pamphlets have no idea how they should mount resistance. They cannot see how it is possible. We aim to show them that each and every one of them is in a position to contribute to the overthrow of this system. It will not be possible to lay the foundations for the swift downfall of this 'government' or even to bring about its downfall through individualistic opposition like an embittered hermit; it can only come about through the conviction and energy of people acting together, people who are agreed on the means that can be used to achieve their goal. We do not have a vast range of means at our disposal, we have only one: PASSIVE RESISTANCE.

The meaning and purpose of passive resistance is to bring down National Socialism and, in this struggle, there is no course, no action that we should fear to take, whatever it may be. National Socialism must be attacked at EVERY weak point, at every chink in its armour. This false state must be brought to an end as soon as possible – in this war, a victory for fascist Germany would have dreadful, unimaginable consequences. The Germans' most immediate concern should not be military victory over Bolshevism, but defeating the National Socialists. This *must* be our most urgent priority. We will illustrate how pressing this is in one of our next pamphlets.

And now, every staunch adversary of National Socialism must ask themselves the question: how can they fight back against the current 'government' most effectively, how can they inflict the most stinging wounds? The answer is, without a doubt: passive resistance. It is clearly impossible for us to provide every individual with direct instructions; we can only give general suggestions; each person must find their own way to put them into practice.

SABOTAGE of arms factories and other strategic operations, sabotage of all meetings, rallies, festivities, organizations, everything that the National Socialist Party brought into being. Any and all hindrance to the smooth operation of the war machine (a machine that is engineered only for war, a war with the sole purpose of saving and preserving the National Socialist Party and its dictatorship). SABOTAGE of all academic and intellectual groups that actively support the continuation of the war – whether they are universities, colleges, laboratories, research institutes or technical firms. SABOTAGE of all cultural events that might raise the fascists' 'prestige' with the people. SABOTAGE of all branches of the arts that have the slightest connection to National Socialism or stand in its service. SABOTAGE of all publications, all newspapers that are in the pay of the 'government', that propagate its ideas and spread the brown lie. Do not give a single penny to street collections (even if they are carried out under the pretence of a charitable cause). This is only a cover. In reality, the sum will not benefit the Red Cross, or the needy. The government does not need this money, it is not financially dependent on these collections — their printing presses are running day and night and can produce all the money they need. But they have to keep the people in a state of tension, held on a tight rein that must never be loosened! Do not donate any scrap metal, any fabric, or anything else! Do your utmost to convince all your acquaintances, from the lower classes too, of the senselessness and futility of continuing this war, of the spiritual and economic enslavement, of the destruction of all moral and religious values, which has been brought about by National Socialism, and to encourage PASSIVE RESISTANCE!

Aristotle's *Politics*: 'A further essential aspect (of tyranny) is seeking to ensure that nothing any subject says or does remains hidden, but rather to spy and eavesdrop on him at every turn ... and moreover to fill the whole world with hatred and to turn friend against friend, the people against the aristocracy, and the wealthy against one another. Thus an aspect of tyrannical discipline is making the subjects poor, so that the guards can be paid and so that they are so concerned about their daily earnings that they have no time or energy to plot a coup-d'état. ... Another aspect of tyranny is the implementation of high income taxes, such as were imposed on Syracuse, for after five years under Dionysius's rule the citizens had happily given up all their wealth in taxes. And the tyrant also has a constant inclination to provoke war...'

Please reproduce this and pass it on!!!

4

F l u g b l ä t t e r   d e r   W e i s s e n   R o s e

IV

Es ist eine alte Weisheit, die man Kindern immer wieder aufs neue predigt, dass wer nicht hören will, fühlen muss. Ein kluges Kind wird sich aber die Finger nur einmal am heissen Ofen verbrennen.

In den vergangenen Wochen hatte Hitler sowohl in Afrika, als auch in Russland Erfolge zu verzeichnen. Die Folge davon war, dass der Optimismus auf der einen, die Bestürzung und der Pessimismus auf der anderen Seite des Volkes mit einer der deutschen Trägheit unvergleichlichen Schnelligkeit anstieg. Allenthalben hörte man unter den Gegnern Hitlers, also unter dem besseren Teil des Volkes, Klagerufe, Worte der Enttäuschung und der Entmutigung, die nicht selten in dem Ausruf endigten: "Sollte nun Hitler doch..?"

Indessen ist der deutsche Angriff auf Aegypten zum Stillstand gekommen, Rommel muss in einer gefährlich exponierten Lage verharren - aber noch geht der Vormarsch im Osten weiter. Dieser scheinbare Erfolg ist unter den grauenhaftesten Opfern erkauft worden, sodass er schon nicht mehr als vorteilhaft bezeichnet werden kann. Wir warnen daher vor j e d e m Optimismus.

Wer hat die Toten gezählt, Hitler oder Göbbels - wohl keiner von beiden. Täglich fallen in Russland Tausende. Es ist die Zeit der Ernte, und der Schnitter fährt mit vollem Zug in die reife Saat. Die Trauer kehrt ein in die Hütten der Heimat, und niemand ist da, der die Tränen der Mütter trocknet. Hitler aber belügt die, deren teuerstes Gut er geraubt und in den sinnlosen Tod getrieben hat.

Jedes Wort, das aus Hitlers Munde kommt, ist Lüge: Wenn er Frieden sagt, meint er den Krieg, und wenn er in frevelhaftester Weise den Namen des Allmächtigen nennt, meint er die Macht des Bösen, den gefallenen Engel, den Satan. Sein Mund ist der stinkende Rachen der Hölle und seine Macht ist im Grunde verworfen. Wohl muss man mit rationalen Mitteln den Kampf wider den nationalsozialistischen Terrorstaat führen; wer aber heute noch an der realen Existenz der dämonischen Mächte zweifelt, hat den metaphysischen Hintergrund dieses Krieges bei weitem nicht begriffen. Hinter dem Konkreten, hinter dem sinnlich wahrnehmbaren, hinter allen sachlichen logischen Ueberlegungen, steht das Irrationale, d.i. der Kampf wider den Dämon, wider den Boten des Antichrists. Ueberall und zu allen Zeiten haben die Dämonen im Dunkeln gelauert auf die Stunde, da der Mensch schwach wird, da er seine ihm von Gott auf Freiheit gegründete Stellung im ordo eigenmächtig verlässt, da er dem Druck des Bösen nachgibt, sich von den Mächten höherer Ordnung loslöst und so, nachdem er den ersten Schritt freiwillig getan, zum zweiten und dritten und immer mehr getrieben wird mit rasend steigender Geschwindigkeit - überall und zu allen Zeiten der höchsten Not sind Menschen aufgestanden, Propheten, Heilige, die ihre Freiheit gewahrt hatten, die auf den Einzigen Gott hinwiesen und mit seiner Hilfe das Volk zur Umkehr mahnten. Wohl ist der Mensch frei, aber er ist wehrlos wider das Böse ohne den wahren Gott, er ist wie ein Schiff ohne Ruder, dem Sturme preisgegeben, wie ein Säugling ohne Mutter, wie eine Wolke, die sich auflöst.

Gibt es, so frage ich Dich, der Du ein Christ bist, gibt es in diesem Ringen um die Erhaltung Deiner höchsten Güter ein Zögern, ein Spiel mit Intrigen, ein Hinausschieben der Entscheidung in der Hoffnung, dass ein anderer die Waffen erhebt, um Dich zu verteidigen? Hat Dir nicht Gott selbst die Kraft und den Mut gegeben zu kämpfen? Wir m ü s s e n das Böse dort angreifen, wo es am mächtigsten ist, und es ist am mächtigsten in der Macht Hitlers.

PAMPHLETS OF THE WHITE ROSE
IV

There is an old and wise saying, which we preach to children time and again, that 'he who will not listen must feel'. However, clever children will burn their fingers on a hot stove only once.

In the past few weeks, Hitler has claimed successes both in Africa and in Russia. The consequence of this is that optimism on the one hand, and dismay and pessimism on the other, have risen among the people with a speed which is wholly unlike the usual German complacency. Everywhere among the opponents of Hitler – that is, among the better part of the people – we hear lamentations, words of disappointment and discouragement, ending not infrequently with the interjection: 'What if Hitler after all...?'

Meanwhile, the German offensive against Egypt has ground to a halt — Rommel must remain in a dangerously exposed position, but the advance in the East still proceeds. This apparent success comes at the most hideous cost to human life, so much so that already it can no longer be claimed as advantageous. We therefore warn against optimism IN ANY FORM.

The first page of the fourth resistance pamphlet of the White Rose, summer 1942.

Who has counted the dead, Hitler or Goebbels? – neither of them, in truth. Thousands fall in Russia every day. It is harvest time, and the Reaper cuts into the ripe crop with broad strokes. Grief settles into the country's cottages, and no one is there to dry the mothers' tears. Hitler, however, lies to those whom he has robbed of their most precious possessions, and driven to a meaningless death.

Every word that comes out of Hitler's mouth is a lie. When he says 'peace', he means 'war', and when he blasphemously invokes the name of the Almighty, he means the power of the Evil One, of the fallen angel, of Satan. His mouth is the stinking maw of Hell, and his power is, at its very essence, corrupt. We must undoubtedly lead a struggle against the National Socialist terror state by rational means, but whoever today still doubts the genuine existence of demonic powers has woefully failed to grasp the metaphysical background of this war. Behind the concrete, behind that which is discernible to the senses, behind all factual, logical considerations, there lies the Irrational, i.e. the fight against the demon, against the messenger of the Antichrist. Everywhere and always, demons have lurked in the darkness, waiting for the day on which man would become weak; the day on which he would forsake his position in the divine order, freely ordained for him by God; the day on which he would surrender to the forces of the Evil One, unbind himself from the powers of a higher order and, having taken the first step of his own volition, be then driven forcibly towards taking the second and third steps at an ever more furious pace. In all places and at all times when man has found himself most in need, men have taken a stand; prophets and saints who, in asserting their freedom, have pointed towards the one and only God and, with His help, beseeched the people to reverse their course. Man is undoubtedly free, but he is defenceless in the face of evil without the one true God: he is like a ship without a rudder, abandoned to the storm; like a nursing child without a mother; like a cloud that disperses.

And so I ask you – you who proclaim yourself Christian – do you waver in this struggle for the preservation of your highest Goods? Is there a calculation, deferring your decision in the hope that someone else will raise their weapons to defend you? Did not God himself endow you with the strength and courage to fight? We MUST make an assault upon evil where it is strongest, and it is strongest in the hands of Hitler.

'So I returned, and considered all the oppressions that are done under the sun: and behold the tears of such as were oppressed, and they had no comforter; and on the side of their oppressors there was power; but they had no comforter.

Wherefore I praised the dead which are already dead more than the living which are yet alive...'

(Ecclesiastes)[2]

Novalis: 'True anarchy is the generative element of religion. Out of the annihilation of all that is positive she raises her glorious head aloft, as the new foundress of the world... Oh, if Europe were to reawaken, and a state of states, a theory of political science, were to confront us! Should hierarchy then ... be the principle of the union of states? Blood will flow over Europe until the nations become aware of the frightful madness which drives them in circles; until, struck by celestial music and pacified, they approach their former altars as a colourful collective, compose works of peace and hold a great festival of peace, hot tears falling upon the smouldering battlefields. Only religion can reawaken Europe, protect the rights of the peoples, and swear Christendom into its peacemaking office, its new splendour visible on earth.'

We want to make clear that the actions of the White Rose are not being done in the service of some foreign power. Although we know that National Socialism's hold on power can only be broken through military force, we are attempting to reawaken the gravely wounded German spirit from within. This rebirth must, however, be preceded by full recognition of the guilt with which the German people have burdened themselves, and by a ruthless battle against Hitler and his all too numerous accomplices, party members, quislings, and so on. The gulf between the better part of society and those who choose to associate with National Socialism must be torn apart with uncompromising brutality. There is no punishment on this earth that would do justice to the crimes of Hitler and his inner circle. But out of love for the coming generations, an example must be set after the end of the war, so that no one will ever feel even the slightest inclination to commit such acts again. Do not forget the petty villains of this regime; remember their names, so that not a single one goes free! After these atrocities, they should not be allowed to get away with switching sides at the last minute and acting as though nothing had happened!

We would like to add for your reassurance that the addresses of White Rose readers are nowhere recorded in writing. The addresses are taken at random from directories.

We will not be silent. We are your bad conscience. The White Rose will never leave you in peace!

Please duplicate and redistribute!

Flugblätter der Widerstandsbewegung in Deutschland.

A u f r u f   a n   a l l e   D e u t s c h e !

Der Krieg geht seinem sicheren Ende entgegen.Wie im Jahre 1918 versucht die deutsche Regierung alle Aufmerksamkeit auf die wachsende U-Bootgefahr zu lenken,während im Osten die Armeen unaufhörlich zurückströmen,im Westen die Invasion erwartet wird. Die Rüstung Amerikas hat ihren Höhepunkt noch nicht erreicht, aber heute schon übertrifft sie alles in der Geschichte seither Dagewesene.Mit mathematischer Sicherheit führt Hitler das deutsche Volk in den Abgrund. H i t l e r   k a n n   d e n   K r i e g   n i c h t   g e w i n n e n ,   n u r   n o c h   v e r l ä n g e r n ! Seine und seiner Helfer Schuld hat jedes Mass unendlich überschritten. Die gerechte Strafe rückt näher und näher !

Was aber tut das deutsche Volk? Es sieht nicht, und es hört nicht.Blindlings folgt es seinen Verführern ins Verderben.Sieg um jeden Preis, haben sie auf ihre Fahne geschrieben. Ich kämpfe bis zum letzten Mann , sagt Hitler - indes ist der Krieg bereits verloren.

Deutsche! Wollt Ihr und Eure Kinder dasselbe Schicksal erleiden, das den Juden widerfahren ist? Wollt Ihr mit dem gleichen Masse gemessen werden, wie Eure Verführer? Sollen wir auf ewig das von aller Welt gehasste und ausgestossene Volk sein? Nein! Darum trennt Euch von dem nationalsozialistischen Untermenschentum! Beweist durch die Tat, dass Ihr anders denkt! Ein neuer Befreiungs- krieg bricht an.Der bessere Teil des Volkes kämpft auf unserer Seite. Zerreisst den Mantel der Gleichgültigkeit, den Ihr um Euer Herz gelegt! Entscheidet Euch, e h ' e s   z u   s p ä t   i s t !

PAMPHLETS OF THE RESISTANCE MOVEMENT IN GERMANY

AN APPEAL TO ALL GERMANS!

The war is heading towards its certain end. Just as in 1918, the German government is trying to channel all attention towards the growing threat of submarines, while in the East the armies are constantly falling back, and in the West the invasion is expected. America's armament has not yet reached its full potential, but even now it exceeds anything ever seen before in history. With mathematical certainty, Hitler is leading the German people into the abyss. HITLER CANNOT WIN THE WAR; HE CAN ONLY PROLONG IT! His guilt and the guilt of his followers continually exceeds all boundaries. Just punishment is nigh!

But what are the Germans doing about it? They refuse to see, and they refuse to hear. Blindly they follow their corrupters into ruin. 'Victory at all costs!', they wrote on their banner. I will fight until the last man, Hitler says – meanwhile, the war is already lost.

The first page of the fifth resistance pamphlet of the White Rose. This was the first pamphlet to dispense with the name 'The White Rose', instead using the title 'Pamphlets of the Resistance Movement in Germany'.

Germans! Do you and your children want to suffer the same fate that befell the Jews? Do you want to be judged by the same measures as those who have corrupted you? Shall we be forever hated and shunned by the whole world? No! So separate yourselves from the subhuman nature of National Socialism! Act – prove that you think differently! A new fight for liberation is at hand. The better part of the people is fighting on our side. Tear off the cloak of indifference that shrouds your heart! Decide – BEFORE IT'S TOO LATE!

Don't believe the National Socialist propaganda that has injected the fear of Bolshevism into your every limb! Don't believe that Germany's salvation is bound to the victory of National Socialism for better or worse! A band of criminals cannot bring about German victory. Break away from everything associated with National Socialism BEFORE IT'S TOO LATE! A terrible, but a righteous judgement is coming to those who holed themselves up in such a cowardly and passive way.

What does the outcome of this war teach us, a war in which it was never our nation that was at stake?

The imperial concept of power, regardless of which side it might come from, needs to be neutralized for all time. A one-sided Prussian militarism should never be allowed to come to power again. Only through the generous collaboration of the European nations can the foundation be built on which a new development will be possible. Every centralizing force, like the one the Prussian state has tried to exercise in Germany and in Europe, must be nipped in the bud. The Germany to come can only be federalist. Only a healthy federalism can bring new life to a weakened Europe. The workers need to be freed from their condition of abject slavery through a level-headed socialism. This delusion of a self-sufficient economy must disappear from Europe. Every nation, every person has a right to the goods of the world!

Freedom of speech, freedom of faith, protection of the individual citizen from the despotism of criminal and violent states: these are the foundations of the new Europe.

Support the resistance movement, *distribute* the pamphlets!

Kommilitoninnen! Kommilitonen!

Erschüttert steht unser Volk vor dem Untergang der Männer von Stalingrad. Dreihundertdreißigtausend deutsche Männer hat die geniale Strategie des Weltkriegsgefreiten sinn- und verantwortungslos in Tod und Verderben gehetzt. Führer, wir danken dir!

Es gärt im deutschen Volk: Wollen wir weiter einem Dilettanten das Schicksal unserer Armeen anvertrauen? Wollen wir den niedrigen Machtinstinkten einer Parteiclique den Rest der deutschen Jugend opfern? Nimmermehr! Der Tag der Abrechnung ist gekommen, der Abrechnung unserer deutschen Jugend mit der verabscheuungswürdigsten Tyrannis, die unser Volk je erduldet hat. Im Namen der ganzen deutschen Jugend fordern wir von dem Staat Adolf Hitlers die persönliche Freiheit, das kostbarste Gut des Deutschen zurück, um das er uns in der erbärmlichsten Weise betrogen hat.

In einem Staat rücksichtsloser Knebelung jeder freien Meinungsäußerung sind wir aufgewachsen. HJ, SA, SS haben uns in den fruchtbarsten Bildungsjahren unseres Lebens zu uniformieren, zu revolutionieren, zu narkotisieren versucht. „Weltanschauliche Schulung" hieß die verächtliche Methode, das keimende Selbstdenken und Selbstwerten in einem Nebel leerer Phrasen zu ersticken. Eine Führerauslese, wie sie teuflischer und bornierter zugleich nicht gedacht werden kann, zieht ihre künftigen Parteibonzen auf Ordensburgen zu gottlosen, schamlosen und gewissenlosen Ausbeutern und Mordbuben heran, zur blinden, stupiden Führergefolgschaft. Wir „Arbeiter des Geistes" wären gerade recht, dieser neuen Herrenschicht den Knüppel zu machen. Frontkämpfer werden von Studentenführern und Gauleiteraspiranten wie Schuljungen gemaßregelt, Gauleiter greifen mit geilen Spässen den Studentinnen an die Ehre. Deutsche Studentinnen haben an der Münchner Hochschule auf die Besudelung ihrer Ehre eine würdige Antwort gegeben, deutsche Studenten haben sich für ihre Kameradinnen eingesetzt und standgehalten. Das ist ein Anfang zur Erkämpfung unserer freien Selbstbestimmung, ohne die geistige Werte nicht geschaffen werden können. Unser Dank gilt den tapferen Kameradinnen und Kameraden, die mit leuchtendem Beispiel vorangegangen sind!

Es gibt für uns nur eine Parole: Kampf gegen die Partei! Heraus aus den Parteigliederungen, in denen man uns politisch weiter mundtot halten will! Heraus aus den Hörsälen der SS- Unter- oder Oberführer und Parteikriecher! Es geht uns um wahre Wissenschaft und echte Geistesfreiheit! Kein Drohmittel kann uns schrecken, auch nicht die Schließung unserer Hochschulen. Es gilt im Kampf jedes einzelnen von uns um unsere Zukunft, unsere Freiheit und Ehre in einem seiner sittlichen Verantwortung bewussten Staatswesen.

Freiheit und Ehre! Zehn lange Jahre haben Hitler und seine Genossen die beiden herrlichen deutsche Worte bis zum Ekel ausgequetscht, abgedroschen, verdreht, wie es nur Dilettanten vermögen, die die höchsten Werte einer Nation vor die Säue werfen. Was ihnen Freiheit und Ehre gilt, haben sie in zehn Jahren der Zerstörung aller materiellen und geistigen Freiheit, aller sittlichen Substanz im deutschen Volk genugsam gezeigt. Auch dem dümmsten Deutschen hat das furchtbare Blutbad die Augen geöffnet, das sie im Namen von Freiheit und Ehre der deutschen Nation in ganz Europa angerichtet haben und täglich neu anrichten. Der deutsche Name bleibt für immer geschändet, wenn nicht die deutsche Jugend endlich aufsteht, rächt und sühnt zugleich, seine Peiniger zerschmettert und ein neues, geistiges Europa aufrichtet.

Studentinnen! Studenten! Auf uns sieht das sieht das deutsche Volk! Von uns erwartet es, wie 1813 die Brechung des Napoleonischen, so 1943 die Brechung des nationalsozialistischen Terrors aus der Macht des Geistes. Beresina und Stalingrad flammen im Osten auf, die Toten von Stalingrad beschwören uns!

„Frisch auf, mein Volk, die Flammenzeichen rauchen!"
Unser Volk steht im Aufbruch gegen die Verknechtung Europas durch den Nationalsozialismus, im neuen gläubigen Durchbruch von Freiheit und Ehre!

FELLOW STUDENTS!

Our people look on deeply shaken at the defeat of our men at Stalingrad. The ingenious strategy of our Great War corporal has hounded three hundred thousand German men senselessly and irresponsibly to death and ruin. Führer, we thank you!

Turmoil is fermenting among the German people: are we to further entrust the fate of our armies to a dilettante? Are we to sacrifice what is left of our German youth to the basest power-grabbing instincts of a party clique? No more!

The day of reckoning has come, the reckoning of Germany's youth with the most heinous tyranny that our people has ever endured. In the name of all German youth, we demand from Adolf Hitler's state the return of our personal freedom, that treasure which Germans hold most dear, and which he has cheated us of in the most wretched of ways.

We have grown up in a state which ruthlessly gags all freedom of expression. The Hitler Youth, the SA and the SS have tried to homogenize, radicalize and anaesthetize us in the most fruitful of our formative years. 'Ideological

The sixth resistance pamphlet of the White Rose. Unlike the other pamphlets, which were double-sided, this one took up just a single side of paper.

Education' is the term they use for their contemptible method of suffocating burgeoning independent thought and self-esteem with a fog of empty rhetoric. The Nazi elite, who could not be any more diabolical or narrow-minded, groom their future party bigwigs in the elite *Ordensburgen* schools to become godless, shameless, unscrupulous, exploitative, murderous scoundrels, the blind and brainless entourage of the Führer. We, 'Workers of the Mind', are the right people to smash this new ruling class. Student leaders and aspiring Gauleiters reprimand front-line soldiers like schoolboys; Gauleiters insult the honour of our female students with lewd jokes. Women studying at Munich University have given a dignified response to the assault on their honour, and their male counterparts have come out in support of them and are standing firm. This is a first step in the fight for our free self-determination, without which spiritual values cannot be forged. We are grateful to the brave students who are lighting the way!

For us there is only one slogan: fight against the party! Get out of the party structures which stifle our political expression! Get out of the lecture halls of the SS and senior leaders and party sycophants! Our goal is true scholarship and real freedom of the mind! There is no threat that can deter us, not even the closure of our universities. It is the duty of each and every one of us to fight for our future, our freedom and honour in a political system conscious of its own moral responsibility.

Freedom and honour! For ten long years, Hitler and his cronies have trivialized, distorted and bled dry these two glorious German words to the point of disgust, as only dilettantes know how, casting a nation's highest ideals before swine. They have shown well enough what freedom and honour mean to them during the ten years in which they have destroyed all material and spiritual freedom, all moral substance of the German people. Even the most dull-witted German has had his eyes opened by the terrible bloodbath, which, in the name of the freedom and honour of the German nation, they have unleashed upon Europe, and unleash anew each day. The German name will remain forever tarnished unless finally the young people of Germany stand up, pursue both revenge and atonement, smite our tormentors, and found a new intellectual Europe.

Students! The German people look to us! The responsibility is ours: just as the power of the spirit broke the Napoleonic terror in 1813, so too will it break the terror of the National Socialists in 1943.

To the east, Berezina and Stalingrad have gone up in flames, the dead of Stalingrad beseech us!

'Rise up, my people, the beacons are aflame!'

Our people are on the verge of breaking free from National Socialism's enslavement of Europe in this new spiritual dawn of freedom and honour!

DRAFT PAMPHLET

Stalingrad!

200,000 German brothers were sacrificed for the prestige of a military fraudster. The humane terms of surrender offered by the Russians were concealed from the sacrificed soldiers. General Paulus was awarded the Knight's Cross with Oak Leaves for this mass murder. High-ranking officers fled the battle of Stalingrad by plane.

Hitler forbade the surrounded men from retreating to the rear troops. Now the blood of 200,000 soldiers, doomed to die, indicts the murderer, Hitler.

Tripoli! It surrendered unconditionally to the English 8th Army. And what did the English do? They left the citizens to continue their lives along the usual tracks. They even let the police and civil servants keep their posts. The one thing they did do thoroughly was to purge the largest Italian colonial city of all false ringleaders and subhumans. With deadly certainty, the annihilating, overwhelming superior power is pressing in from all sides. If Paulus was not willing to surrender, then Hitler is hardly likely to. Even if there is no escape left for him. And will you allow yourselves to be deceived like the 200,000 men at Stalingrad who defended their posts in vain? To be massacred, or sterilized, or robbed of your children? Roosevelt, the most powerful man in the world, said on 26 January 1943 in Casablanca: We are waging this war of annihilation not against peoples, but against political systems. We are fighting until an unconditional surrender is reached. Do you really need to give it any more thought before you make up your mind?

The lives of millions are now at stake. Must Germany share the same fate as Tripoli? All of Germany is now surrounded, just as Stalingrad was. Must every German be sacrificed to the harbinger of hatred and wanton destruction? To the one who tortured the Jews to death, who exterminated half of Poland, and who tried to destroy Russia, to the one who took from you your freedom, peace, domestic happiness, hope and joy, and gave you inflated currency in return? That must not, that cannot be! Hitler and his regime must fall so that Germany may live on. The choice is yours: Stalingrad and ruin, or Tripoli and hope for the future. And when you have chosen, act.

TIMELINE OF EVENTS

24 October 1893	Kurt Huber is born in Chur, Switzerland.
28 July 1914	Outbreak of World War I.
16 September 1917	Alexander Schmorell is born in Orenburg, Russia.
2 January 1918	Willi Graf is born in Kuchenheim near Euskirchen, Germany.
22 September 1918	Hans Scholl is born in Ingersheim, Germany.
11 November 1918	World War I ends.
6 November 1919	Christoph Probst is born in Murnau, Germany.
9 May 1921	Sophie Scholl is born in Forchtenberg, Germany.
30 January 1933	Adolf Hitler becomes chancellor of Germany.
15 September 1935	Nuremberg Laws passed.
12 March 1938	Annexation of Austria.
30 September 1938	Munich Agreement is signed.
1 October 1938	German troops march into the Sudetenland.
15 March 1939	German troops invade Czechoslovakia.

23 August 1939	German–Soviet non-aggression pact is signed.
1 September 1939	Germany invades Poland. World War II begins.
22 June 1941	Germany invades the Soviet Union.
1 September 1941	Star of David becomes compulsory for all Jews over the age of 6.
7 December 1941	Japanese attack on Pearl Harbour.
11 December 1941	Germany declares war on the USA.
20 January 1942	Wannsee Conference to discuss the 'Final Solution' is held in Berlin.
May 1942	Sophie Scholl begins her studies at the Ludwig Maximilian University in Munich.
27 June–12 July 1942	First four White Rose pamphlets are printed and distributed.
22 July 1942	Deportation of Jews from the Warsaw Ghetto to Treblinka begins.
23 July 1942	Hans Scholl, Willi Graf and Alexander Schmorell leave Munich for the Eastern Front.
3 August 1942	Robert Scholl is sentenced to four months in prison for defaming Adolf Hitler.
1 November 1942	Hans Scholl, Willi Graf and Alexander Schmorell return to Germany.
January 1943	Fifth pamphlet is distributed.
13 January 1943	Gauleiter's speech in the Ludwig Maximilian University in Munich

	on the occasion of the 470th anniversary of its founding.
14 January 1943	The Casablanca Conference begins.
2 February 1943	The Sixth Army is defeated at the Battle of Stalingrad.
3 February 1943	Hans Scholl, Willi Graf and Alexander Schmorell graffiti Munich buildings with anti-Nazi slogans.
8 February 1943	Hans Scholl, Alexander Schmorell and Willi Graf meet Falk Harnack in Munich. Scholl, Graf and Schmorell graffiti Munich buildings with anti-Nazi slogans.
9 February 1943	Harnack meets with Scholl, Schmorell, Graf and Huber. Disagreement between Huber and Harnack. Further disagreement between Huber and Schmorell/ Scholl over the phrase 'the ranks of our glorious Wehrmacht'.
15 February 1943	Hans Scholl, Willi Graf and Alexander Schmorell graffiti Munich buildings with anti-Nazi slogans.
18 February 1943	Hans Scholl and Sophie Scholl distribute copies of the pamphlets at Munich University. They are arrested. Goebbels delivers his 'total war' speech in Berlin. Willi Graf and his sister Anneliese are arrested in Munich.

20 February 1943	Christoph Probst is arrested in Innsbruck.
22 February 1943	First White Rose trial. The accused are Hans Scholl, Sophie Scholl and Christoph Probst. Hans Scholl, Sophie Scholl and Christoph Probst are executed.
24 February 1943	Alexander Schmorell is arrested in Munich.
27 February 1943	Kurt Huber is arrested in Munich.
3 April 1943	Willi Bollinger is tried for assisting the White Rose activities in Saarbrücken.
19 April 1943	Second White Rose trial. The accused are Alexander Schmorell, Willi Graf, Kurt Huber, Eugen Grimminger, Heinz Bollinger, Helmut Bauer, Hans Hirzel, Franz Josef Müller, Heinrich Guter, Gisela Schertling, Katharina Schüddekopf, Traute Lafrenz, Susanne Hirzel and Falk Harnack.
13 July 1943	Alexander Schmorell and Kurt Huber are executed. Third White Rose trial. The accused are Wilhelm Geyer, Harald Dohrn, Josef Söhngen and Manfred Eickemeyer.
12 October 1943	Willi Graf is executed.
6 June 1944	Normandy landings.
20 July 1944	Unsuccessful attempt to assassinate Adolf Hitler by Claus von Stauffenberg and other conspirators.

13 October 1944	Hans Leipelt, Marie-Luise Jahn and others are tried for their involvement in the White Rose.
29 January 1945	Hans Leipelt is executed.
8 May 1945	Germany surrenders to the Allies.

NOTES

Unless otherwise stated, all translations are my own.

INTRODUCTION

1. Joseph Goebbels, *Die Tagebücher von Joseph Goebbels*, Volume I: *Aufzeichnungen 1923–1941*, ed. Elke Fröhlich, K.G. Saur, Munich, 1987, p. 190.
2. Anthony Beevor, *Stalingrad*, Penguin, London, 2011, p. 399.
3. Joseph Goebbels, '"Total War", 18 February 1943', in Randall L. Bytwerk (ed. and trans.), *Landmark Speeches of National Socialism*, Texas A&M University Press, College Station TX and London, 2008, pp. 114–40.
4. Albert Speer, *Inside the Third Reich*, trans. Richard and Clara Winston, Simon & Schuster, New York, 1970, p. 257.
5. Goebbels, '"Total War"', p. 136.
6. Joseph Goebbels, '"People, Rise Up, and Storm, Break Loose", 18 February 1943', in Bytwerk (ed. and trans.), *Landmark Speeches of National Socialism*, pp. 112–13, p. 112.
7. Cited in Simone König, *Die Gedenkveranstaltungen zur Erinnerung an den Widerstand der Weißen Rose an der Ludwig-Maximilians-Universität München von 1945 bis 1968*, Utz, Munich, 2017, p. 32.
8. Ulrich Chaussy and Gerd R. Ueberschär, *'Es lebe die Freiheit!': Die Geschichte der Weißen Rose und ihrer Mitglieder in Dokumenten und Berichten*, Fischer, Frankfurt am Main, 2013, p. 84.
9. 'Sentence of Hans and Sophie Scholl and Christoph Probst', in Inge Scholl, *The White Rose: Munich, 1942–1943*, trans. Arthur R. Schultz, Wesleyan University Press, Middletown CT, 1983, pp. 114–19, p. 117.
10. Chaussy and Ueberschär, *'Es lebe die Freiheit!'*, p. 517.
11. Christiane Moll, 'Acts of Resistance: The White Rose in the Light of New Archival Evidence', in M.E. Geyer and J.W. Boyer (eds),

Resistance against the Third Reich: 1933–90, University of Chicago Press, Chicago IL and London, 1994, pp. 173-201, p. 177.

12. Miriam Gebhardt, *Die Weiße Rose: Wie aus ganz normalen Deutschen Widerstandskämpfer wurden*, dtv, Munich, 2017, p. 33.

13. Ibid., p. 30.

14. Frank McDonough, *Sophie Scholl: The Real Story of the Woman Who Defied Hitler*, History Press, Stroud, 2010, pp. 24-5.

15. Hinrich Siefken, '"Die Weiße Rose" and Russia', *German Life and Letters* 47, 1994, pp. 14-43, p. 29.

16. McDonough, *Sophie Scholl*, p. 91.

17. Siefken, '"Die Weiße Rose" and Russia', p. 26.

18. Inge Jens, *At the Heart of the White Rose: Letters and Diaries of Hans and Sophie Scholl*, trans. J. Maxwell Brownjohn, Plough Publishing House, Walden NY, 2017, p. 351.

19. Christiane Moll, 'Alexander Schmorell und Christoph Probst: Eine biographische Einführung', in *Alexander Schmorell, Christoph Probst: Gesammelte Briefe*, ed. Christiane Moll, Lukas, Berlin, 2011, pp. 23-283, p. 162.

20. Traute Lafrenz, 'Augenzeugenbericht', in Inge Scholl (ed.), *Die Weiße Rose*, Fischer, Frankfurt am Main, 2016, pp. 131-8, p. 131.

21. Cited in Moll, 'Alexander Schmorell und Christoph Probst: Eine biographische Einführung', p. 185.

22. *Flugblätter* can also be translated as leaflets, flyers, broadsheets or handbills.

23. See Patrick Brugh, *Gunpowder, Masculinity, and Warfare in German Texts 1400-1700*, University of Rochester Press, Rochester NY, 2019, p. 97.

24. Moll, 'Eine biographische Einführung', p. 188.

25. See Corina L. Petrescu, *Against all Odds: Models of Subversive Spaces in National Socialist Germany*, Peter Lang, Bern and New York, 2010, p. 116.

26. Cited in Moll, 'Alexander Schmorell und Christoph Probst: Eine biographische Einführung', p. 189.

27. 'Vernehmungen von Hans Scholl', in Chaussy and Ueberschär, *'Es lebe die Freiheit!'*, pp. 255-307, pp. 295-6.

28. The text to which he referred was *Romanzen vom Rosenkranz* (1852). See Jakob Knab, *Ich schweige nicht: Hans Scholl und die Weiße Rose*, wbg Thiess, Darmstadt, 2018, p. 137.

29. See Hinrich Siefken, 'Introduction', in Hinrich Siefken (ed.), *Die Weiße Rose und ihre Flugblätter: Dokumente, Texte, Lebensbilder, Erläuterungen*, University of Manchester Press, Manchester, 1993, pp. 1–12, pp. 6–7; Knab, *Ich schweige nicht*, pp. 137–9.

30. Chaussy and Ueberschär, *'Es lebe die Freiheit!'*, p. 248.

31. Moll, 'Alexander Schmorell und Christoph Probst: Eine biographische Einführung', p. 191.

32. Ibid., p. 192.

33. Michael Verhoeven and Mario Krebs, *Die Weiße Rose: Der Widerstand Münchener Studenten gegen Hitler – Informationen zum Film*, Fischer, Frankfurt am Main, 1982, p. 124.

34. 'Pamphlets of the White Rose I', trans. Louise Mayer-Jacquelin and Poppy Robertson.

35. Richard Overy, *The Bombing War: Europe 1939–1945*, Allen Lane, London, 2014, pp. 339–40.

36. Mark Clapson, *The Blitz Companion: Aerial Warfare, Civilians and the City since 1911*, University of Westminster Press, London, 2019, p. 85.

37. See Alexander Schmidt, 'The Liberty of the Ancients? Friedrich Schiller and Aesthetic Republicanism', *History of Political Thought*, vol. 30, no. 2, Summer 2009, pp. 286–314.

38. See Siefken, *Die Weiße Rose*, p. 36; Moll, 'Alexander Schmorell und Christoph Probst: Eine biographische Einführung', p. 156.

39. Gebhardt, *Die Weiße Rose*, p. 199.

40. Karl Alt, 'Augenzeugebericht', in Scholl (ed.), *Die Weiße Rose*, pp. 188–91, p. 191.

41. Cited in Clara Huber, 'Kurt Hubers Schicksalsweg', in Clara Huber (ed.), *'...der Tod... war nicht vergebens': Kurt Huber zum Gedächtnis*, Nymphenburger Verlag, Munich, 1986, pp. 25–66, p. 54.

42. 'Pamphlets of the White Rose II', trans. Pauline Gümpel, Eve Mason and Timothy Powell.

43. Gebhardt, *Die Weiße Rose*, p. 13.

44. Knut Walf, 'Reading and Meaning of Daoist Texts in Nazi Germany', in Raoul David Findeisen, Gad C. Isay, Amira Katz-Goehr et al. (eds), *At Home in Many Worlds: Reading, Writing and Translating from Chinese and Jewish Cultures*, Harrassowitz Verlag, Wiesbaden, 2009, pp. 149–63, p. 151.

45. 'Pamphlets of the White Rose III', trans. Zoë Aebischer, Harry Smith and Madeleine Williamson-Sarll.

46. Siefken, *Die Weiße Rose*, p. 43.

47. 'Pamphlets of the White Rose IV', trans. Adam Mazarelo, Emily Rowland and Amy Wilkinson.

48. On Haecker, see Hinrich Siefken, 'Die Weiße Rose und Theodor Haecker: Widerstand im Glauben', in Hinrich Siefken (ed.), *Die Weiße Rose: Student Resistance to National Socialism 1942/1943: Forschungsergebnisse und Erfahrungsberichte*, University of Nottingham Monographs in the Humanities, vol. VII, Nottingham, 1991, pp. 117–46. See also Paul Shrimpton, *Conscience before Conformity: Hans and Sophie Scholl and the White Rose Resistance in Nazi Germany*, Gracewing, Leominster, 2017, pp. 160–61, 229–31.

49. Theodor Haecker, *Journal in the Night*, trans. Alexander Dru, Pantheon, New York, 1950, p. 220.

50. Knab, *Ich schweige nicht*, pp. 133–4.

51. Siefken, 'Introduction', in *Die Weiße Rose*, p. 7.

52. Wolfgang Huber (ed.), *Die Weiße Rose: Kurt Hubers letzte Tage*, Utz, Munich, 2018, p. 45.

53. Petrescu, *Against all Odds*, p. 166.

54. 'Pamphlets of the Resistance Movement in Germany', trans. Ilona Clayton and Ro Crawford.

55. Lafrenz, 'Augenzeugenbericht', p. 132.

56. This story is told by Inge Scholl in *The White Rose*, pp. 32–4, though it has been disputed elsewhere. See, for example, Barbara Beuys, *Sophie Scholl: Biografie*, Hanser, Munich, 2010, p. 363.

57. For an excellent and detailed discussion of the role of this period, and of Russian culture, in the development of the White Rose, see Siefken, '"Die Weiße Rose" and Russia'.

58. Ibid., pp. 21–3.

59. Willi Graf, Diary, 23 July 1942, in *Willi Graf: Briefe und Aufzeichnungen*, ed. Anneliese Knoop-Graf and Inge Jens, Fischer, Frankfurt am Main, 1994, p. 44; trans. Lucy Buxton, Beth Molyneux and Greta Simpson.

60. Verhoeven and Krebs, *Die Weiße Rose*, p. 135.

61. Willi Graf, Diary, 26 July 1942, in *Willi Graf: Briefe und Aufzeichnungen*, p. 44; trans. Buxton, Molyneux and Simpson.

62. Hans Scholl, letter, 27 July 1942, in *Hans Scholl, Sophie Scholl: Briefe und Aufzeichnungen*, ed. Inge Jens, Fischer Taschenbuch Verlag, Frankfurt am Main, 1988, pp. 104–5; trans. Holly Abrahamson, Sam Davis, Benjy Fortna and Alice Hopkinson-Woolley.

63. Knab, *Ich schweige nicht*, p. 145.

64. His 'Russian friend' was Alexander Schmorell. Letter, 17 August 1942, in Jens (ed.), *Hans Scholl, Sophie Scholl: Briefe und Aufzeichnungen*, pp. 106–7.

65. Hans Scholl, Diary, 28 August 1942, in *Hans Scholl und Sophie Scholl: Briefe und Aufzeichnungen*, p. 114; trans. Abrahamson, Davis, Fortna and Hopkinson-Woolley.

66. McDonough, *Sophie Scholl*, pp. 102–3.

67. Hans Scholl, Diary, 28 August 1942, in *Hans Scholl und Sophie Scholl: Briefe und Aufzeichnungen,* pp. 126–7; trans. Abrahamson, Davis, Fortna and Hopkinson-Woolley.

68. Christoph Probst, letter, 18 October 1942, in *Gesammelte Briefe*, p. 802; trans. Luke Cooper, Jonah Cowen and Thomas Lyne.

69. Sophie Scholl, letter, 7 November 1942, in Sophie Scholl and Fritz Hartnagel, *Damit wir uns nicht verlieren: Briefwechsel 1937–1943*, ed. Thomas Hartnagel, Fischer, Frankfurt am Main, 2006, pp. 424–5; trans. Lydia Ludlow, Amira Ramdani and Amelia Farley.

70. Wolfgang Benz, *Die Weiße Rose: 100 Seiten*, Reclam, Stuttgart, 2017, p. 70.

71. W. Huber (ed.), *Die Weiße Rose*, p. 51.

72. Willi Graf, Diary, 13 January 1943, in *Willi Graf: Briefe und Aufzeichnungen*, p. 99.

73. Moll, 'Alexander Schmorell und Christoph Probst: Eine biographische Einführung', p. 212.

74. Benz, *Die Weiße Rose*, p. 28.

75. 'Pamphlets of the Resistance Movement in Germany', trans. Clayton and Crawford.

76. Moll, 'Alexander Schmorell und Christoph Probst: Eine biographische Einführung', p. 216.

77. Ibid., pp. 217–18.

78. W. Huber (ed.), *Die Weiße Rose*, pp. 56–7.

79. Gebhardt, *Die Weiße Rose*, p. 248; Sibylle Bassler, *Die Weiße Rose: Zeitzeugen erinnern sich*, Rowohlt, Reinbek, 2006, p. 11.

80. Chaussy and Ueberschär, *'Es lebe die Freiheit!'*, pp. 78–9.

81. Ibid., p. 79. See also Falk Harnack, 'Augenzeugenbericht', in I. Scholl, *Die Weiße Rose*, pp. 147–64, pp. 151–2.

82. Cited in W. Huber (ed.), *Die Weiße Rose*, pp. 54–5. See also Chaussy and Ueberschär, *'Es lebe die Freiheit!'*, pp. 80–81.

83. 'Fellow students!', trans. Sophie Bailey and Finn Provan.

84. Paul Giesler, 13 January 1943, University of Munich, cited in Russell

Freedman, *We Will Not Be Silent: The White Rose Student Resistance Movement That Defied Adolf Hitler*, Clarion Books, New York, 2016, p. 65.

85. Petra Umlauf, *Die StudentInnen an der Universität München 1926 bis 1945: Auslese, Beschränkung, Indienstnahme, Reaktionen*, De Gruyter, Berlin and Boston MA, 2015, p. 689.

86. Cited in Benz, *Die Weiße Rose*, p. 82.

87. W. Huber (ed.), *Die Weiße Rose*, p. 51.

88. Goebbels, '"Total War", 18 February 1943', p. 139.

89. Richard Hanser, *A Noble Treason: The Story of Sophie Scholl and the White Rose Revolt against Hitler*, Ignatius Press, San Francisco CA, 2012, p. 266.

90. Kurt Huber, 'Verteidigung', in W. Huber (ed.), *Die Weiße Rose*, pp. 104–22, p. 112.

91. Gebhardt, *Die Weiße Rose*, p. 250.

92. Ibid., p. 249.

93. Knab, *Ich schweige nicht*, p. 181.

94. See Chaussy and Überschar, *'Es lebe die Freiheit!'*, pp. 86–7.

95. Richard Harder, 'Schriftgutachten', in Chaussy and Ueberschär, *'Es lebe die Freiheit'*, pp. 48–57.

96. Ibid., p. 57. See also Annette Dumbach and Jud Newborn, *Sophie Scholl and the White Rose*, Oneworld Publications, Oxford, 2007, p. 58.

97. Chaussy and Ueberschär, *'Es lebe die Freiheit!'*, p. 53.

98. Gebhardt, *Die Weiße Rose*, p. 247.

99. 'Stalingrad!', trans. Sophie Bailey, Ro Crawford, Eve Mason, Timothy Powell, Poppy Robertson, Emily Rowland and Amy Wilkinson.

100. Christoph Probst, letter, 22 February 1943, in *Gesammelte Briefe*, p. 887; trans. Cooper, Cowen and Lyne.

101. Chaussy and Ueberschär, *'Es lebe die Freiheit!'*, p. 128.

102. Moll, 'Acts of Resistance', pp. 175–7. The interrogation documents are reproduced in Chaussy and Ueberschär, *'Es lebe die Freiheit!'*, pp. 213–326, 341–496.

103. Robert D. Rachlin, 'Roland Freisler and the Volksgerichtshof: The Court as an Instrument of Terror', in Alan E. Steinweis and Robert D. Rachlin (eds), *The Law in Nazi Germany: Ideology, Opportunism, and the Perversion of Justice*, Berghahn Books, New York, 2013, p. 81.

104. Robert Mohr, 'Augenzeugenbericht', in I. Scholl, *Die Weiße Rose*, pp. 171–81, p. 177.

105. Leo Samberger, 'Augenzeugenbericht', in I. Scholl, *Die Weiße Rose*, pp. 183–7, p. 184.

106. I. Scholl, *The White Rose*, p. 114.

107. McDonough, *Sophie Scholl*, p. 147.

108. Mertz, *Christoph Probst*, p. 28.

109. Cited in I. Scholl, *The White Rose*, p. 148.

110. Scholl and Hartnagel, *Damit wir uns nicht verlieren*, p. 464.

111. McDonough, *Sophie Scholl*, p. 147.

112. Fritz Hartnagel, letter, 22 February 1943, in Scholl and Hartnagel, *Damit wir uns nicht verlieren*, p. 457; trans. Sibylle Bandilla, Genevieve Jeffcoate and Finn Provan.

113. The original telegram is available to view on the website of the German State Archive, www.bundesarchiv.de/DE/Content/Virtuelle-Ausstellungen/Sophie-Und-Hans-Scholl-Zum-Tode-Verurteilt-Am-22-02-1943/sophie-und-hans-scholl-zum-tode-verurteilt-am-22-02-1943.html; accessed 15 April 2021.

114. Scholl and Hartnagel, *Damit wir uns nicht verlieren*, p. 461.

115. Moll, 'Alexander Schmorell und Christoph Probst: Eine biographische Einführung', p. 251.

116. Thomas Mertz, *Christoph Probst: Ein Student der 'Weißen Rose'*, Paulinus, Trier, 2020, pp. 134–5, p. 135.

117. Christoph Probst, letter, 22 February 1943, in *Gesammelte Briefe*, pp. 888–9;. trans. Cooper, Cowen and Lyne.

118. Gebhardt, *Die Weiße Rose*, p. 118.

119. Knab, *Ich schweige nicht*, p. 199.

120. Magdalena Scholl, letter, 25 February 1943, in Scholl and Hartnagel, *Damit wir uns nicht verlieren*, p. 466.

121. Moll, 'Alexander Schmorell und Christoph Probst: Eine biographische Einführung', pp. 254–62.

122. *Münchner Neueste Nachrichten*, 24 February 1943, reproduced in *Kurt Huber: Stationen seines Lebens in Dokumenten und Bildern*, ed. Kurt-Huber-Gymnasium, Kurt-Huber-Gymnasium, Gräfeling, 1986, p. 61.

123. Robert M. Zoske, *Flamme sein! Hans Scholl und die Weiße Rose: Eine Biografie*, C.H. Beck, Munich, 2018,, p. 202.

124. W. Huber (ed.), *Die Weiße Rose*, p. 64.

125. Moll, 'Alexander Schmorell und Christoph Probst: Eine biographische Einführung', p. 273.

126. Chaussy and Ueberschär, '*Es lebe die Freiheit!*', p. 497.

127. Benz, *Die Weiße Rose*, p. 71. While he served his sentence, his Jewish wife Jenny was deported to Auschwitz, where she was murdered.
128. Zoske, *Flamme sein!*, p. 231.
129. Ibid.
130. Dumbach and Newborn, *Sophie Scholl*, p. 167.
131. C. Huber, '...der Tod... war nicht vergebens', p. 40. See also W. Huber (ed.), *Die Weiße Rose*, pp. 80–83.
132. Sibylle Bassler, *Die Weiße Rose: Zeitzeugen erinnern sich*, Rowohlt, Reinbek, 2006, p. 28.
133. Moll, 'Alexander Schmorell und Christoph Probst: Eine biographische Einführung', p. 275.
134. See Robert Loeffel, *Family Punishment in Nazi Germany: Sippenhaft, Terror and Myth*, Palgrave Macmillan, Basingstoke, 2012, p. 36.
135. W. Huber, 'Die Vollstreckung des Urteils', in *Die Weiße Rose*, p. 232. See also C. Huber, '...der Tod... war nicht vergebens', p. 61.
136. Dumbach and Newborn, *Sophie Scholl*, p. 180.
137. Petrescu, *Against all Odds*, p. 161.
138. C. Huber, '...der Tod... war nicht vergebens', p. 60.
139. Cited in Chaussy and Ueberschär, 'Es lebe die Freiheit!', p. 514.
140. Ibid.
141. Ibid., pp. 506–9.
142. Ibid.
143. See Emily Oliver, '"Deutsche Hörer!": News of the White Rose on the BBC German Service', in Alexandra Lloyd (ed.), *The White Rose: Reading, Writing, Resistance*, Taylor Institution Library, Oxford, 2019, pp. 47–61, p. 48.
144. Thomas Mann, *Deutsche Hörer! 55 Radiosendungen nach Deutschland von Thomas Mann*, Bermann-Fischer Verlag, Stockholm, 1945, p. 94.
145. See especially Christian Ernst, *Die Weiße Rose – Eine deutsche Geschichte?: Die öffentliche Erinnerung an den Widerstand in beziehungsgeschichtlicher Perspektive*, V&R, Göttingen, 2018.
146. Robert M. Zoske, *Es reut mich nichts: Porträt einer Widerständigen*, Propyläen, Berlin, 2020, p. 293.
147. For a fascinating discussion of the book and its reception, see Joanne Sayner, *Women without a Past? German Autobiographical Writings and Fascism*, Rodopi, Amsterdam and New York, 2007, pp. 75–119.
148. See Further Reading below.

149. This included the publication in German of writings by Hans Scholl, Sophie Scholl, Kurt Huber and Willi Graf. In English, selected letters by Hans and Sophie Scholl were published as *At the Heart of the White Rose: Letters and Diaries of Hans and Sophie Scholl*, ed. Inge Jens, trans. J. Maxwell Brownjohn, Harper & Row, New York, 1987.

150. The installation of this sculpture in Walhalla was not uncontroversial. See Katie Rickard 'Memorializing the White Rose Resistance Group in Post-War Germany', in Bill Niven and Chloe Paver (eds), *Memorialization in Germany since 1945*, Palgrave Macmillan, Basingstoke, 2010, pp. 157–68.

151. 'Der Geschwister Scholl Preis', https://geschwister-scholl-preis.de (accessed 10 January 2021).

152. Haecker, *Journal in the Night*, p. 220.

153. Helmuth James Graf von Moltke, 'The Case of Hans Scholl, Maria Scholl, Adrian Probst, Professor Kurt Huber', in Kristina Kargl, *Die Weiße Rose: Defizite einer Erinnerungskultur: Einfluss und Wirkung des Exils auf die Publizität der Münchner Widerstandsgruppe*, Allitera Verlag, Munich, 2014, pp. 202–5, p. 204.

154. See Gerd R. Ueberschär, *Für ein anderes Deutschland: Der deutsche Widerstand gegen den NS-Staat 1933–1945*, Fischer, Frankfurt am Main, 2005, pp. 156–64.

155. See ibid, pp. 133–40.

156. Hanser, *A Noble Treason*, p. 272.

157. Dumbach and Newborn, *Sophie Scholl*, p. 185.

158. Eleanor F. Rathbone, 'Preface', in William Bayles, *Seven Were Hanged*, Victor Gollancz, London, 1945, pp. 3–4, p. 4.

BIOGRAPHICAL SKETCHES

1. Barbara Beuys, *Sophie Scholl: Biografie*, Hanser, Munich, 2010, p. 137.

2. Cited in Ernest M. Wolf, *Blick auf Deutschland: Kleine Skizzen zur deutschen Kulturkunde*, Scribner, New York, 1966, p. 113.

3. Sophie Scholl, letter, 9 April 1940, in Scholl and Hartnagel, *Damit wir uns nicht verlieren*, p. 160; trans. Lydia Ludlow, Amira Ramdani and Amelia Farley.

4. Moll, 'Alexander Schmorell und Christoph Probst: Eine biographische Einführung', p. 219.

5. Cited in Chaussy and Ueberschär, *'Es lebe die Freiheit!'*, p. 254.

6. Zoske, *Flamme sein!*, p. 231.

7. Dumbach and Newborn, *Sophie Scholl*, pp. 26–7.

8. I. Scholl, *The White Rose*, p. 8.
9. Knab, *Ich schweige nicht*, pp. 48–9.
10. Hans Scholl, letter, 18 March 1942, in *Hans Scholl and Sophie Scholl*, p. 101.
11. Cited in Chaussy and Ueberschär, *'Es lebe die Freiheit'*, p. 118.
12. Gebhardt, *Die Weiße Rose*, p. 103.
13. Moll, 'Alexander Schmorell und Christoph Probst: Eine biographische Einführung', p. 77.
14. Ibid., p. 80.
15. Cited in Gebhardt, *Die Weiße Rose*, pp. 107–8.
16. Ibid., p. 112.
17. Moll, 'Eine biographische Einführung', p. 238.
18. Cited in Chaussy and Ueberschär, *Es lebe die Freiheit!*, p. 313.
19. Christoph Probst, letter, 22 February 1943, in *Gesammelte Briefe*, pp. 888–9; trans. Cooper, Cowen and Lyne.
20. Moll, 'Alexander Schmorell und Christoph Probst: Eine biographische Einführung', p. 32.
21. McDonough, *Sophie Scholl*, p. 52.
22. Alexander Schmorell, letter, 13 July 1943, in *Gesammelte Briefe*, p. 530; trans. James Cutting, Rachel Herring and Gerda Krivaite.
23. W. Huber (ed.), *Die Weiße Rose*, p. 67.
24. Dumbach and Newborn, *Sophie Scholl*, p. 86.
25. C. Huber, 'Kurt Hubers Schicksalsweg', in *'...der Tod... war nicht vergebens'*, pp. 25–66, p. 25.
26. Dumbach and Newborn, *Sophie Scholl*, p. 89.
27. Gebhardt, *Die Weiße Rose*, p. 145.
28. W. Huber (ed.), *Die Weiße Rose*, p. 16.
29. Walter H. Rubsamen, 'Kurt Huber of Munich', *Musical Quarterly*, vol. 30, no. 2, April 1944, pp. 226–33, pp. 228–31.
30. Ibid., p. 231.
31. Dumbach and Newborn, *Sophie Scholl*, p. 90.
32. W. Huber (ed.), *Die Weiße Rose*, p. 51.
33. Zoske, *Flamme sein!*, p. 229.
34. Cited in C. Huber, *'...der Tod... war nicht vergebens'*, p. 42.
35. Cited in Klaus Drobisch, *Wir schweigen nicht: Eine Dokumentation über den antifaschistischen Kampf Münchner Studenten 1942/43*, Union-Verlag, Berlin, 1968, p. 134.
36. Cited in I. Scholl, The *White Rose*, p. 127.
37. Cited in C. Huber, *'...der Tod... war nicht vergebens'*, p. 78.

38. Cited in W. Huber (ed.), *Die Weiße Rose*, pp. 228–30.

39. Cited in ibid., p. 231.

40. Another sibling died in infancy. See Peter Goergen, *Willi Graf: Ein Weg in den Widerstand*, Röhrig Universitätsverlag, St. Ingbert, 2009, p. 18.

41. Benz, *Die Weiße Rose*, p. 54.

42. Anneliese Knoop-Graf and Inge Jens (eds), *Briefe und Aufzeichnungen*, Fischer, Frankfurt am Main, 1994, p. 248.

43. Siefken, '"Die Weiße Rose" and Russia', p. 26.

44. McDonough, *Sophie Scholl*, p. 91.

45. Willi Graf, Diary, 13 June 1942, in *Willi Graf*, p. 37; trans. Lucy Buxton, Beth Molyneux and Greta Simpson.

46. Gebhardt, *Die Weiße Rose*, p. 227; Moll, 'Alexander Schmorell und Christoph Probst: Eine biographische Einführung', pp. 215–16.

47. Moll, 'Alexander Schmorell und Christoph Probst: Eine biographische Einführung', p. 216.

48. Knoop-Graf, 'Vorbemerkung zum Tagebuch', in *Willi Graf*, p. 27.

49. Zoske, *Flamme sein!*, p. 230.

50. Ibid.

51. Willi Graf, letter, 12 October 1943, in *Willi Graf*, p. 201; trans. Buxton, Molyneux and Simpson.

52. Ibid, p. 200.

53. Ibid.

54. Goergen, *Willi Graf*, p. 201.

55. Heinrich Hamm, 'Augenzeugenbericht', in Drobisch, *Wir schweigen nicht*, p. 181.

56. Cited in Chaussy and Ueberschär, *'Es lebe die Freiheit!'*, p. 166.

THE WHITE ROSE PAMPHLETS

1. English translations originally published in *The White Rose: Reading, Writing, Resistance*, ed. Alexandra Lloyd, Taylor Institution Library, Oxford, 2019, pp. 111–94.

2. The White Rose attribute the quotation to the Book of Proverbs (*Sprüche*) though it is in fact taken from Ecclesiastes 4.1.

BIBLIOGRAPHY

FURTHER READING AND VIEWING

YOUNG ADULT FICTION

Kaye, Hayden, *The Girl Who Said No to the Nazis: Sophie Scholl and the Plot against Hitler*, Pushkin Children's Books, London, 2020.

Wilson, Kip, *White Rose*, Versify, New York, 2019.

FICTIONALIZED ACCOUNTS

Barratt, Amanda, *The White Rose Resists: A Novel of the German Students who Defied Hitler*, Kregel Publications, Grand Rapids MI, 2020.

Bayles, William, *Seven were Hanged*, Camelot Press, London and Southampton, 1945

Lehmann, Alexandra, *With You There Is Light: Based on the True Story about Sophie Scholl and Fritz Hartnagel*, L&L Media, Columbia SC, 2017.

Neumann, Alfred, *Six of Them*, trans. Anatol Murad, Macmillan, New York, 1945.

GRAPHIC NOVELS

Ciponte, Andrea Grosso, *Freiheit! The White Rose Graphic Novel*, Plough Publishing House, Walden NY, 2021.

NON-FICTION

Axelrod, Toby, *Hans and Sophie Scholl: German Resisters of the White Rose*, Rosen Publishing Group, New York, 2001.

Dumbach, Annette, and Jud Newborn, *Sophie Scholl and the White Rose*, Oneworld, Oxford, 2007.

Freedman, Russell, *We Will Not Be Silent: The White Rose Student Resistance Movement That Defied Adolf Hitler*, Clarion Books, New York, 2016.

Hanser, Richard, *A Noble Treason: The Story of Sophie Scholl and the White Rose Revolt against Hitler*, Ignatius Press, San Francisco CA, 2012.

Jens, Inge (ed.), *At the Heart of the White Rose: Letters and Diaries of Hans and*

Sophie Scholl, trans. J. Maxwell Brownjohn, Plough Publishing House, Walden NY, 2017.

Lloyd, Alexandra (ed.), *The White Rose: Reading, Writing, Resistance*, Taylor Institution Library, Oxford, 2019.

McDonough, Frank, *Sophie Scholl: The Real Story of the Woman Who Defied Hitler*, History Press, Stroud, 2010.

Melon, Ruth Bernadette, *Journey to the White Rose*, Dog Ear Publishing, Indianapolis IN, 2007.

Moll, Christiane, 'Acts of Resistance: The White Rose in the Light of New Archival Evidence', in M.E. Geyer and J.W. Boyer (eds), *Resistance against the Third Reich: 1933–90*, University of Chicago Press, Chicago IL and London, 1994.

Petrescu, Corina L., 'The Open Protest of the *Scholl–Schmorell–Kreis*', in *Against All Odds: Models of Subversive Spaces in National Socialist Germany*, Peter Lang, Bern, 2010.

Sachs, Ruth Hanna, *White Rose History,* Volume 1: *Coming Together: January 31, 1933–April 30 1942*, Exclamation Publishers, Phoenixville PA, 2003.

Sahgal, Lara, and Toby Axelrod, *Hans and Sophie Scholl*, Rosen Publishing Group, New York, 2016

Scholl, Inge, *The White Rose: Munich, 1942–1943*, Wesleyan University Press, Middletown CT, 1983.

Schott, Gerhard, *Die Weiße Rose, Student Resistance in the Third Reich, 1943: Memorial Exhibition*, Munich University Library, Munich, 1983.

Shrimpton, Paul, *Conscience before Conformity: Hans and Sophie Scholl and the White Rose Resistance in Nazi Germany*, Gracewing, Leominster, 2017.

Siefken, Hinrich, 'Introduction', in *Die Weiße Rose: Student Resistance to National Socialism, 1942-1943: Forschungsergebnisse und Erfahrungsberichte: A Nottingham Symposium*, University of Nottingham, 1991.

——, 'Introduction', in *Die Weiße Rose und ihre Flugblätter: Dokumente, Texte, Lebensbilder, Erläuterungen*, University of Manchester Press, Manchester, 1993.

——, '"Die Weiße Rose" and Russia', *German Life and Letters* 47, 1994, pp. 14-43.

Smith,David I., 'Teaching (and Learning from) the White Rose', in David M. Moss and Terry A. Osborn (eds), *Critical Essays on Resistance in Education*, Peter Lang, New York, 2010, pp. 67-81.

Stern, J.P., 'The White Rose', in H. Siefken (ed.), *Die Weiße Rose Student Resistance to National Socialism 1942/1943: Forschungsergebnisse und*

Erfahrungsberichte, University of Nottingham, 1991, pp. 11–36.

Tolansky, Ethel, and Helena Scott, *Sophie Scholl and the White Rose: Resistance to the Nazis*, Catholic Truth Society, London, 2012.

Vinke, Hermann, *The Short Life of Sophie Scholl*, Harper & Row, New York, 1980.

The White Rose, Weiße Rose Stiftung, Munich, 2006.

FILM

Rothemund, Marc (dir.), *Sophie Scholl: The Final Days*, X Verleih, 2005.

Seybold, Katrin, *No! Witnesses of Resistance in Munich 1933–45*, Basis-Film, 1998.

——, *The Resisters: Testimony of the White Rose*, Basis-Film, 2008.

Verhoeven, Michael (dir.), *Die Weiße Rose*, CCC Film, 1982.

REFERENCES

Alexander, V.S., *The Traitor*, Kensington Publishing, London, 2020.

Bald, D., *'Die Weisse Rose': Von der Front in den Widerstand*, Aufbau, Berlin, 2003.

Bassler, S., *Die Weiße Rose: Zeitzeugen erinnern sich*, Rowohlt, Reinbek, 2006.

Beevor, A., *Stalingrad*, Penguin, London, 2017.

Benz, W., *Die Weiße Rose: 100 Seiten*, Reclam, Stuttgart, 2017.

——, and W.H. Pehle (eds), *Lexikon des deutschen Widerstandes*, Fischer, Frankfurt am Main, 2001.

Beuys, B., *Sophie Scholl: Biografie*, Hanser, Munich, 2010.

Brugh, P., *Gunpowder, Masculinity, and Warfare in German Texts, 1400–1700*, University of Rochester Press, Rochester NY, 2019.

Bussmann, W., *Der deutsche Widerstand und die Weiße Rose*, Hueber, Munich, 1968.

Chaussy, U., and G.R. Ueberschär, *'Es lebe die Freiheit!': Die Geschichte der Weißen Rose und ihrer Mitglieder in Dokumenten und Berichten*, Fischer, Frankfurt am Main, 2013.

Chramov, I., *Die russische Seele der 'Weißen Rose'*, Helios, Orenburg, 2001.

——, *Alexander Schmorell: Gestapo-Verhörprotokolle, Februar–März 1943, RGWA 1361K-1-8808*, Helios, Orenburg, 2005.

Clapson, M., *The Blitz Companion: Aerial Warfare, Civilians and the City since 1911*, University of Westminster Press, London, 2019.

Diem, V., *Die Freiheitsaktion Bayern: Ein Aufstand in der Endphase des NS-Regimes*, Laßleben, Kallmünz, 2013.

Drobisch, K., *Wir schweigen nicht! Eine Dokumentation über den antifaschistischen Kampf Münchener Studenten 1942/1943*, Union Verlag, Berlin, 1983.

Dumbach, A., and J. Newborn, *Sophie Scholl and the White Rose*, Oneworld Publications, Oxford, 2007.

Ellermeier, B., *Sophie Scholl: Lesen ist Freiheit!*, bene!, Munich, 2018.

Ernst, C., *Die Weiße Rose – Eine deutsche Geschichte?: Die öffentliche Erinnerung an den Widerstand in beziehungsgeschichtlicher Perspektive*, V&R, Göttingen, 2018.

Freedman, R., *We Will Not Be Silent: The White Rose Student Resistance Movement That Defied Adolf Hitler*, Clarion Books, New York, 2016.

Fürst-Ramdohr, L., *Freundschaften in der Weißen Rose*, Munich, Geschichtswerkstatt Neuhausen, 1995.

Gebhardt, M., *Die Weiße Rose: Wie aus ganz normalen Deutschen Widerstandskämpfer wurden*, dtv, Munich, 2017.

Goebbels, J., *Die Tagebücher von Joseph Goebbels*, Volume 1: *Aufzeichnungen 1923–1941*, ed. Elke Fröhlich, K.G. Saur, Munich, 1987.

——, '"Total War", 18 February 1943', in *Landmark Speeches of National Socialism*, ed. and trans. R.L. Bytwerk, Texas A&M University Press, College Station TX and London, 2008, pp. 114–40.

Goergen, P., *Willi Graf: Ein Weg in den Widerstand*, Röhrig Universitätsverlag, St. Ingbert, 2009.

Graf, W., *Briefe und Aufzeichnungen*, ed. Anneliese Knoop-Graf and Inge Jens, Fischer, Frankfurt am Main, 1994.

Haecker, T., *Tag- und Nachtbücher 1939–1945*, Kösel Verlag, Munich, 1947.

——, *Journal in the Night*, trans. Alexander Dru, Pantheon, New York, 1950.

Hanser, R., *A Noble Treason: The Story of Sophie Scholl and the White Rose Revolt against Hitler*, Ignatius Press, San Francisco CA, 2012.

Harnack, F., 'Augenzeugenbericht', in I. Scholl, *Die Weiße Rose*, Fischer, Frankfurt am Main, 2016, pp. 147–64

Hikel, C., *Sophies Schwester: Inge Scholl und die Weiße Rose*, Oldenbourg Verlag, Munich, 2013.

Holzberg, N., 'Lycurgus in Leaflets and Lectures: The Weiße Rose and Classics at Munich University, 1941–45', *Arion: A Journal of Humanities and the Classics* 23, 2015, pp. 33–52.

Huber, C. (ed.), '...der Tod... war nicht vergebens': Kurt Huber zum Gedächtnis*, Nymphenburger Verlag, Munich, 1986.

Huber, W. (ed.), *Die Weiße Rose: Kurt Hubers letzte Tage*, Utz, Munich, 2018.

Jens, I. (ed.), *Hans Scholl, Sophie Scholl: Briefe und Aufzeichnungen*, Fischer, Frankfurt am Main, 1988.

———, *At the Heart of the White Rose: Letters and Diaries of Hans and Sophie Scholl*, trans. J. Maxwell Brownjohn, Plough, Walden NY, 2017.

Kargl, K., *Die Weisse Rose: Defizite einer Erinnerungskultur: Einfluss und Wirkung des Exils auf die Publizität der Münchner Widerstandsgruppe*, Allitera Verlag, Munich, 2014,

Knab, J., *Ich schweige nicht: Hans Scholl und die Weiße Rose*, Wbg Thiess, Darmstadt, 2018.

König, S., *Die Gedenkveranstaltungen zur Erinnerung an den Widerstand der Weißen Rose an der Ludwig-Maximilians-Universität München von 1945 bis 1968*, Utz, Munich, 2017.

Kurt-Huber-Gymnasium (ed.), *Kurt Huber: Stationen seines Lebens in Dokumenten und Bildern*, Kurt-Huber-Gymnasium, Gräfeling, 1986.

Lafrenz, T., 'Augenzeugenbericht', in Inge Scholl (ed.), *Die Weiße Rose*, Fischer, Frankfurt am Main, 2016, pp. 131–8.

Loeffel, R., *Family Punishment in Nazi Germany: Sippenhaft, Terror and Myth*, Palgrave Macmillan, Basingstoke, 2012.

Mann, T., *Deutsche Hörer! 55 Radiosendungen nach Deutschland von Thomas Mann*, Bermann-Fischer Verlag, Stockholm, 1945.

Marcuse, H., 'Remembering The White Rose: (West) German Assessments, 1943–1993', *Soundings*, vol. 22, no. 9, 1994, pp. 25–38.

McDonough, F., *Sophie Scholl: The Real Story of the Woman who Defied Hitler*, History Press, Stroud, 2010.

Melon, R.B., *Journey to the White Rose*, Dog Ear Publishing, Indianapolis IN, 2007.

Mertz, T., *Christoph Probst: Ein Student der 'Weißen Rose'*, Paulinus, Trier, 2020.

Moll, C., 'Acts of Resistance: The White Rose in the Light of New Archival Evidence', in M.E. Geyer and J.W. Boyer (eds), *Resistance against the Third Reich: 1933–90*, University of Chicago Press, London and Chicago IL, 1994, pp. 173–201.

———, 'Alexander Schmorell und Christoph Probst: Eine biographische Einführung', in C. Moll (ed.), *Alexander Schmorell, Christoph Probst: Gesammelte Briefe*, Lukas, Berlin, 2011, pp. 23–283.

———(ed.), *Alexander Schmorell, Christoph Probst: Gesammelte Briefe*, Lukas, Berlin, 2011.

Moltke, H.J. von, *Briefe an Freya 1939–1945*, Beck, Munich, 1991.

Overy, R., *The Bombing War: Europe 1939–1945*, Allen Lane, London, 2014.

Petrescu, C.L., *Against all odds: Models of Subversive Spaces in National Socialist Germany*, Peter Lang, Bern and New York, 2010.

Petry, C., *Studenten aufs Schafott: Die Weiße Rose und ihr Scheitern*, Piper, Munich, 1968.

Rathbone, E.F., 'Preface', in William Bayles, *Seven were Hanged*, Victor Gollancz, London, 1945, pp. 3–4.

Richards-Wilson, S., 'Faith under Fire: Willi Graf of the White Rose', www.kritische-ausgabe.de/artikel/faith-under-fire; accessed 15 January 2021.

Rickard, K., 'Memorializing the White Rose Resistance Group in Post-War Germany', in Bill Niven and Chloe Paver (eds), *Memorialization in Germany since 1945*, Palgrave Macmillan, Basingstoke and New York, 2010, pp. 157–68.

Rubsamen, W.H., 'Kurt Huber of Munich', *Musical Quarterly*, vol. 30, no. 2, April 1944, pp. 226–33.

Sayner, J., *Women without a Past?: German Autobiographical Writings and Fascism*, Rodopi, Amsterdam and New York, 2007.

Schmidt, A., 'The Liberty of the Ancients? Friedrich Schiller and Aesthetic Republicanism', *History of Political Thought*, vol. 30, no. 2, Summer 2009, pp. 286–314

Scholl, I., *The White Rose: Munich, 1942–1943*, trans. Arthur R. Schultz, Wesleyan University Press, Middletown CT, 1983.

——, *Die Weiße Rose*, Fischer, Frankfurt am Main, 2016.

Scholl, S., and F. Hartnagel, *Damit wir uns nicht verlieren: Briefwechsel 1937–1943*, ed. Thomas Hartnagel, Fischer, Frankfurt am Main, 2006.

Schumann, R., *Leidenschaft und Leidensweg: Kurt Huber im Widerspruch zum Nationalsozialismus*, Droste, Düsseldorf, 2007.

Sherratt, Y., *Hitler's Philosophers*, Yale University Press, New Haven CT, 2013.

Shrimpton, P., *Conscience before Conformity: Hans and Sophie Scholl and the White Rose Resistance in Nazi Germany*, Gracewing, Leominster, 2018.

Siefken, H. (ed.), *Die Weiße Rose Student Resistance to National Socialism 1942/1943: Forschungsergebnisse und Erfahrungsberichte*, University of Nottingham, 1991.

——, 'Die Weiße Rose und Theodor Haecker: Widerstand im Glauben', in Hinrich Siefken (ed.), *Die Weiße Rose Student Resistance to National Socialism 1942/1943: Forschungsergebnisse und Erfahrungsberichte*, University of Nottingham, 1991, pp. 117–46.

——, *Die Weiße Rose und ihre Flugblätter: Dokumente, Texte, Lebensbilder, Erläuterungen*, University of Manchester Press, Manchester, 1993.

——, '"Die Weiße Rose" and Russia', *German Life and Letters* 47, 1994, pp. 14-43.

Speer, A., *Inside the Third Reich*, trans. R. and C. Winston, Simon & Schuster, New York, 1970.

Stern, J.P., 'The White Rose', in H. Siefken (ed.), *Die Weiße Rose Student Resistance to National Socialism 1942/1943: Forschungsergebnisse und Erfahrungsberichte*, University of Nottingham, 1991, pp. 11-36.

Sturms, F., *Die Weiße Rose: Die Geschwister Scholl und der Studentische Widerstand*, Marix Verlag, Wiesbaden, 2013.

Tolansky, E., and H. Scott, *Sophie Scholl and the White Rose: Resistance to the Nazis*, Catholic Truth Society, London, 2012.

Ueberschär, G.R., *Für ein anderes Deutschland: Der deutsche Widerstand gegen den NS-Staat 1933-1945*, Fischer, Frankfurt am Main, 2006.

Umlauf, P., *Die StudentInnen an der Universität München 1926 bis 1945: Auslese Beschränkung, Indienstnahme, Reaktionen*, De Gruyter, Berlin and Boston MA, 2015.

Vargo, M.E., *Women of the Resistance: Eight who Defied the Third Reich*, McFarland, Jefferson NC, 2012.

Verhoeven, M., and M. Krebs, *Die Weiße Rose: Der Widerstand Münchener Studenten gegen Hitler – Informationen zum Film*, Fischer, Frankfurt am Main, 1982.

Vinke, H., *Das kurze Leben der Sophie Scholl*, Ravensburger, Ulm, 1987.

——, *Fritz Hartnagel: Der Freund von Sophie Scholl*, Arche, Zurich and Hamburg, 2005.

Walf, K., 'Reading and Meaning of Daoist Texts in Nazi Germany', in Raoul David Findeisen, Gad C. Isay, Amira Katz-Goehr et al. (eds), *At Home in Many Worlds: Reading, Writing and Translating from Chinese and Jewish Cultures*, Harrassowitz Verlag, Wiesbaden, 2009, pp. 149-63.

Wittenstein, G., 'The White Rose: A Commitment', in J.J. Michaelczyk (ed.), *Confront! Resistance in Nazi Germany*, Peter Lang, New York, 2004.

Wolf, E.M., *Blick auf Deutschland: Kleine Skizzen zur deutschen Kulturkunde*, Scribner, New York, 1966.

Zoske, R.M., *Es reut mich nichts: Porträt einer Widerständigen*, Propyläen, Berlin, 2020.

——, *Flamme sein! Hans Scholl und die Weiße Rose: Eine Biografie*, C.H. Beck, Munich, 2018.

——, *Sehnsucht nach dem Lichte: Zur religiösen Entwicklung von Hans Scholl: Unveröffentlichte Gedichte, Briefe und Texte*, Utz, Munich, 2014.

CREDITS

ii detail of p. 27.
viii Bundesarchiv, Bild 183-J05235/photo Ernst Schwahn
9 Institut fur Zeitgeschichte, Munich/Nachlass Inger Aicher-Scholl, II/ED 474/83
17 Bundesarchiv Berlin-Lichterfelde
27 © George (Jürgen) Wittenstein/akg-images
49 © bpk/Deutsches Historisches Museum/Sebastian Ahlers
53 © Alexandra Lloyd
60 © George (Jürgen) Wittenstein/akg-images
64 © akg-images/Interfoto
68 © akg-images/Interfoto
72 Private collection/Familie Schmorell
76 Private collection
80 Bayerisches Hauptstaatarchiv
84 © Christopher Bade, Boston
90 Bundesarchiv Berlin-Lichterfelde
96 Bundesarchiv Berlin-Lichterfelde
102 Bundesarchiv Berlin-Lichterfelde
108 Bundesarchiv Berlin-Lichterfelde
114 Bundesarchiv Berlin-Lichterfelde
118 Bundesarchiv Berlin-Lichterfelde

Thanks are due to the following for kind permission to reproduce quotations in translation:

Wolfgang Huber, from W. Huber (ed.), *Die Weiße Rose: Kurt Hubers letzte Tage*, Utz, Munich, 2018.

Christiane Moll and Lukas Verlag, from C. Moll (ed.), *Alexander Schmorell, Christoph Probst: Gesammelte Briefe*, Lukas, Berlin, 2011.

Langen Müller Verlag, from C. Huber (ed.), *'...der Tod... war nicht vergebens': Kurt Huber zum Gedächtnis*, Nymphenburger Verlag, Munich, 1986.

Scripture quotations are from The Authorized (King James) Version. Reproduced by permission of the Crown's Patentee, Cambridge University Press.

INDEX